OH YES IT IS!

KEVIN JOHNS

with Peter Read

y Lolfa

First impression: 2008

The publisher acknowledges the support
of the Welsh Books Council

Cover photograph: Marc Lloyd Evans
Cover design: Y Lolfa

ISBN: 9781847710611

Published, printed and bound in Wales
by Y Lolfa Cyf., Talybont, Ceredigion SY24 5HE
website www.ylolfa.com
e-mail ylolfa@ylolfa.com
tel 01970 832 304
fax 832 782

Contents

Acknowledgements

A huge thank you to the legions of friends who have helped me on this journey, especially to my dear friend and wife Rosie, who is my rock and has the patience of Job.

My children, Owain and Bethan, who are my two greatest pals and a thousand times more talented than I.

My Mam and Dad, who have always supported and encouraged me.

To the three Petes in our lives: Pete Williams, who is a joy to know and brightens up the darkest of days; Peter Read for giving me Vicar Joe and creating the most wonderful of lines; and Peter Richards for taking a risk with Kev Johns! All three have been a constant encouragement.

Phil Evans, who has never tired of giving his support and love.

Steve Barnes who has had more dramas and crises with me in the office than a man should have outside of marriage!

Gary and Gerald at the Grand, and Richard Dodge, who is always a phonecall away.

Our good friends Quintin Young – for constant friendship – and Rob Clarke, who can make the greatest doubter believe in themselves.

Finally to my extended family at Swansea Sound, Fluellen, Riverside in Gorseinon, and all the lovely people I have encountered on this journey.

KEVIN JOHNS

CHAPTER 1

Making Sense of It All

HELLO, THIS IS ME... Oh Yes It Is... Kevin Johns!

The performer, actor, pantomime dame, radio broadcaster, football fanatic and the guy with the mike at all of Swansea City's home games. The boy from Plasmarl in Swansea who has ended up chatting, laughing and crying with some of the biggest names in sport and showbiz. I have also worked with some of the most displaced people in society and been a chaplain to footballers, supporters and their families.

I am a Swansea Jack, born within the sound of St Mary's bells. I grew up in Plasmarl. From the age of six I lived in Sex Terrace. Not many people can make that claim, and I don't suppose I can really. The street was actually called Essex Terrace, but whoever put up the drain pipe at Number One Essex Terrace must have had a great sense of humour, because he covered the first two letters. So, as far as visitors were concerned, I did live in Sex Terrace.

I was born on 13 April 1961 in Beresford Nursing Home in the Uplands, which I suppose was quite something for a Plasmarl family. My early years were spent in Bartley Terrace where we lived with my great-grandmother who was a dressmaker and a hard worker. As a single mother, she had brought up her son, and for various reasons, brought up my mother as well. My mum saw her parents but was nurtured by her grandmother and a network of aunts. I was the only child in my family but that never bothered me as I had a great number of friends.

When I was six we moved just a few streets away to Essex Terrace. It was a great place to grow up. For me, it was a boys' street. There were a few girls there who were older than us boys, and therefore, unobtainable.

With my best friends, Wayne and Andrew, we would play all kinds of games, although for all of us football was the main thing. Near where I lived was a whole collection of fields called the Mount, where we played mammoth games of football, often totalling fifteen-a-side. Our street would take on any other street that dared to come and challenge the boys of Sex Terrace.

If we weren't playing football, we would spend the morning collecting large shoots called Sally Rhubarbs, which we would then use to fight with in the afternoon. If you were hit by one it really hurt. It was important not to cry, because I thought being hit by one of them was what growing up was all about.

People from outside Swansea don't realise the importance we locals attach to the community we come from. When I am in Swansea, I will say I am from Plasmarl, rather than Swansea. In reality, I will say I am half Plasmarl and half Hafod, as the latter is where my father and his family originate. To be authentic, I would not say Hafod, as any self-respecting local would drop the aitch and say, "'Afod!" Growing up in those two places gave me a real sense of belonging to a close-knit community and also a love for stories, which I have never lost.

My grandmother lived in the Hafod, on Aberdyberthi Street. For generations in Wales there has been a tradition to encourage children to do their party piece for friends and relatives who then give them money. I learnt how to spell the street name very early on in life because I figured that I could make money out of it. My grandmother would say, "Mrs Williams, you come and listen to our Kevin now. He's a very clever boy. He can spell where we live. I don't know where he gets it from and I don't know who he takes after, but he's a genius. Come in here, now, into the house, but don't look at the mess." I would say, "But Nan, you've been cleaning the house since six o'clock this morning."

"Shut up, mun. *She* doesn't know that," my grandmother would say. She was the kind of woman, who if she booked someone to steam clean the settee, would spend the morning cleaning it herself, so no one would accuse her of having a dirty settee.

So Mrs Williams would come in, hear me spell the street, smile and then give me money. I suppose you could say it was my first professional gig in the world of entertainment. My friend, Paul Steer, lived on Terrace Road in Mount Pleasant. There is no glory in spelling Terrace Road. He had to dance to 'Lily The Pink' to earn his money!

My grandparents on my father's side, Iris and Ernie, lived at No. 61, Aberdyberthi Street. Outside, there was a telegraph pole. I'd often be running out of the door with my gran in hot pursuit. I'd look back, concentrating too much on whether she was closing the gap, and would run slap bang into the telegraph pole.

Every city has a particular story about one of their streets. The Aberdyberthi Street story runs along these lines. Two local men had been down the Hafod Inn for a drink one night. The pub was called the LA by residents, which was nothing to do with California or Los Angeles. It stood for the 'Lower 'Afod'. Just as it took me a long time to work out the meaning of LA, it took me even longer to discover the USA was a local reference to the 'Uther Side of 'Afod' and not the United States of America.

Anyway, the two men came out of the public house worse for wear. Near the legendary telegraph pole was a pothole. One of them fell down the hole and banged his head against the pole. His friend telephoned for an ambulance. In a drunken voice he slurred his way through a conversation with a female receptionist.

"My friend, Alan, is unconscious and has hit his head on a telegraph pole." She asked him where he was and he replied, "I am in the 'Afod." When she asked him for a fuller description of where they were, he said, "I am on Aberdyberthi Street." On being asked to spell it, he said, "Of course, love. I'm sorry, I've lived here all my life. I forget that some people can't spell it."

From further conversation, he established that she was from Newport, so she needed all the help he could offer. In that slow, laborious manner that most drunks use when they are trying to be understood by the sober, he began, "A… B… E… " Then he corrected himself, "A… B… A… " Trying again, he started, "A… B… " After a pause, he said, "Oh, forget it love. I'll drag him around to Neath Road and the ambulance can pick him up there."

My father was a tanker driver for BP, and like many people in his locality, he worked very hard. Many is the time he has worked a night shift, come home in the morning, had a couple of hours sleep and then said, "Come on, let's go to London for the day." On other occasions he'd take us to Gower where we would play on the beach, swim in the sea and have fun jumping on and off sand dunes. In family folklore the immortal story is still told about my mother standing on top of the dune not prepared to jump. Every one was shouting, "Go on, Wendie. Jump!" Still protesting, she stayed where she was; then the sand gave way and she completely disappeared from view. As always happens in such a crisis the rest of the group were laughing so uncontrollably, we were all powerless to give her a helping hand.

I learnt so much from both my parents. My mother didn't go to work until I was in my early teens, when she became a social worker. I think I developed my thirst for social justice from all the stories she told me and the care and concern she showed for those clients who needed help. Like my mother, my father was also concerned about others and was often involved in local campaigns. They taught to me fight for what was right and recognise what was wrong in society. They also helped me to see the importance of respecting all people.

Driving a tanker for BP is quite a dangerous job, but it has given my father an encyclopaedic knowledge of roads. It's funny that even today when ever I am on the roads my dad will phone me. Inevitably he will say the same thing: "Where are you?"

"Margam."

"You won't be long then," he'll say. He makes that statement irrespective of my reply. Margam, Monmouth, Scotch Corner, Charles De Gaulle Airport in Paris will all be given the same response, "Oh, you won't be long then."

On one occasion I had been speaking at an event in Newtown in Mid Wales. Stopping at a garage in Llandrindod Wells, I said to my wife, Rosie, and our children, "Whatever you want in the way of sweets, get them now, because I'm not stopping again until we hit civilisation," which to me is Cross Hands. So we went into the garage shop and bought crisps, sweets, sandwiches, magazines and comics. In fact we bought so much I didn't have the cash to pay, so I had to write a cheque.

As I drove over the mountain towards Llandovery, I remembered why I had gone into the garage in the first place. What reminded me was the little light on the dashboard which said I had run out of diesel. I knew I would be fine as far as Llandovery, because it is mainly downhill, but then I would be in trouble. There was a garage in Llandovery, but in those days it was only open two days a week and the rest of the week it was a chemist's shop! When we got there, I had to ring my father, because you can't run a car on paracetemol. He answered the phone, and on hearing where I was, gave me the legendary retort, "Oh, you won't be long then."

"I'll be longer than you think. The car won't work."

"What's wrong with it?"

"I don't know," I answered. "I've done all the blokey things. I got out of the car, opened the bonnet, scratched my head, fiddled with a few things, but it still won't go. Nothing's happening." He said, "You haven't run out of diesel, have you?" I said, "Dad, you're a genius." He got out of bed, got some diesel and drove all the way to Llandovery. I suppose that's what dads do, and I have always been grateful for his and my mother's support throughout my life.

Growing up as a child in Essex Terrace, I was convinced that the Bogey Man lived in our house. I used to hear him at night and I came to believe that he lived in the loft. There was only one way into the loft which was through a trap door in the bathroom. It was a nightmare going to the toilet. I would look over my shoulder and check in the mirror that I hadn't gone missing, and I would also look out in case he was behind me.

One Saturday, my parents took me shopping in Swansea city centre. They bought me a pasty from Eynon's and a comic from Smith's. When I got home I took my comic to the only place to read such material. As I sat on the loo, enjoying the exploits of the wonderful Roy of the Rovers, I heard this noise above me. I looked up and saw that the loft trap door was open. The rule in our house was that the loft door was only opened on two occasions: December to get the Christmas decorations down and the beginning of

January to put them back up for next year. I was reading Roy of the Rovers in the middle of July. It could mean only one thing. The Bogey Man had decided to come and get Kevin Johns! There were fifteen stairs between me and the front door, four stairs out of the bathroom, a turn, and then another eleven to safety. I navigated the fifteen stairs in two giant steps of fear. I got down to the bottom so quickly I didn't have time to adjust my trousers. They were still down around my ankles. I screamed for my mother. She ran out of the kitchen.

"What's the matter with you?"

"The Bogey Man is coming to get me," I screeched.

"You fool," she replied, "Your father's fixing the tank in the loft." It was a terrible thing to do without telling his son, and it could have left a scar on his fifteen-year-old boy for life!

My mother has been a wonderful influence on my life with her common sense reactions to crises. She is one of the original Welsh mams who would say to me when I was a child climbing trees, "If you fall and break your legs, don't you come running to me!"

Of course, the other great influence and fellow traveller in my roller coaster life has been my wife, Rosie. When I arrived at Elim Bible College as a student in 1982, I was determined to make my time there more successful than it had been at London Bible College, where I had previously studied. I was equally determined not to look for a relationship as I had just broken up with a long-term girlfriend. One of the first things I did at the college was organise a performance group. When I first met Rosie through the group, we just clicked. I heard her say to a friend that she liked ballet but she had never been. I thought to myself, "If I am going to ask this girl out, I don't want to be knocked back, so, as they say in Wales, I must 'pull a flanker'." I studied the London papers and discovered that the Royal Winnipeg Ballet was coming to Sadler's Wells. I bought student rate tickets for the Saturday matinee and then contacted Rosie to say as nonchalantly as I could, "I happen to have two tickets here to see the Royal Winnipeg Ballet at Sadler's Wells. Would you like to come with me?" She said she would, and so we went to see the show and then I treated her to a Wimpy afterwards. I was a perfect gentleman and slowly but surely after that we grew together.

We started going out with each other on 4 November 1982. I proposed the following January. We became officially engaged in the April of 1983 and married in February 1986. She is my rock and we have a huge amount of fun together. Our son, Owain, was born in April 1987 and Bethan was born in March 1990. I am proud of both of my children, and love Rosie, Bethan and Owain to bits.

Having introduced the major characters, perhaps it's time to embark on the journey together. A journey with highs and lows, plus certainties and question marks. From an early age I wanted to be an entertainer and then in adolescence, whilst a pupil at Dynevor Secondary School, a religious experience sent me in the direction of the Church and full-time ministry. Since then my life has seen me with feet in several diverse camps: football, acting, pantomime, broadcasting and football chaplaincy.

This battle between football and religion, the secular and the spiritual, has pursued me all my life. In secondary school I was dogged by the dilemma of whether to listen to the voice that told me to aim for the performing arts or to follow the growing call to enter the Church. It is a battle that has raged throughout my life and this book is the story of how I have listened to and followed both.

My early life as an entertainer reflects those two worlds of religion and entertainment, as I began my life as a children's entertainer or clown, whilst I was a student at London Bible College.

CHAPTER 2

Clowning Around

I FIND IT QUITE DIFFICULT to talk or write about the period of my life when I performed as a clown. I suppose it is all to do with the perceptions of the British people towards the art of the clown and the fact that once you are pigeonholed as a particular type of performer, it is very difficult to break out and develop your skills in another sector of the Arts. In America and other parts of Europe it is a very different story. There, clowning is a highly-respected part of the business of the entertainer. Cirque du Soleil, which originated in France, is huge across the world, and what they produce is accepted as an exciting art form.

Despite the tendency of many to relegate clowning to the bottom division, one could argue that pantomime and much contemporary comedy owe their roots to it. Tommy Cooper with his fez is an obvious example of someone who perfected clowning into a class act. Ken Dodd with his tickling stick and the Diddymen also seemed to make great use of it in his performances. It's also interesting that when I appeared in *Goldilocks and the Three Bears* in 2000-01 at Swansea Grand Theatre, the show was hailed as a great innovative success because it combined the two traditions of pantomime and clowning.

While I was more of a children's entertainer who happened to dress up as a clown, I have to admit to having great respect for the Eastern European clowns who you see entertaining in circuses. By comparison, British circus clowns tend to be fill-ins between one act and the next. Their European counterparts, on the other hand, take the art form to a completely different level. As someone who believes strongly in animal rights, I am thrilled that all the major circuses now ban the use of animals and I think this has helped the clown's act to become a more important part of circus entertainment.

I never intended to be a clown! After leaving school, my first year in London Bible College was a difficult struggle. From an early age I'd believed I would eventually make my living as an entertainer. I was thirteen when I first decided that the only thing I wanted to do with my adult life was be a performer. That certainty was seriously challenged by my belief in school that I was called to some form of Christian ministry. However, the belief in that Christian calling was now taking a battering in theological college. Was I really cut out for a life in the Church? Those doubts were bolstered by the responses of contacts and friends. Many people who knew or met me would raise their eyebrows whenever I mentioned the Church. For most people I was a million miles wide of their image of a clergyman. One friend said to me, "You're the last person I'd ever have thought of as a minister."

This constant battle affected me greatly whilst I was at the

Bible College. I don't think the staff there saw the best in me because I was never sure what I should do. Should it be the Church or the world of entertainment? The battle never affected my faith; it was more an issue of what I wanted to do for the rest of my life.

At the end of my first year in Bible College I moved back home. I had not been in Swansea very long when I received a phone call from Brian Sullivan who was the Entertainments Officer at Swansea City Council. Brian wanted someone to work at the Patti Pavilion, stage managing the summer indoor shows, overseeing the twice-weekly putting competitions at Southend Gardens, and distributing leaflets to Swansea families and tourists advertising children's events. I got involved as stage manager of the afternoon shows, but unfortunately the audiences were rather disappointing.

I realised we had a huge number of leaflets sitting around the place. I asked Brian if he would like me to distribute them, and when he said yes, I had to think of the best way. I came up with the idea that I would dress as a clown and take to the streets. I bought a huge pair of trousers from a charity shop in Morriston and my mother sewed a few patches on them. I also bought a pair of brightly-coloured boots and a felt bowler hat, and slapped on a bit of make up. A friend of mine, Christine, dressed up as Noddy, and we were ready for all-comers!

One afternoon I had a large number of children around me, telling them about the summer shows and doing a few idiotic things with balloons, when a man approached.

"Do you do this for a living?" he asked. One thing you

learn in show business is that you must never say no. If they ask you, "Can you speak French?" you say, "Oui." If they ask, "Can you ride a horse?" you reply, "Giddee up!" And if they ask you, as this man was, "Do you do this for a living?" then you say, "Yes," as they clearly want you to do a job.

The job he offered was to entertain families outside the old Cinderella's nightclub near the Pier in Mumbles. The shows were to be every Saturday night throughout the summer months and my fee was to be £15 for two hours, which were split between the Amusement Arcade and the Sea Horse Grill.

I suppose £15 doesn't sound much these days, but I was excited by the fact that this was my first job as an entertainer. Since my youth I had watched as many comic performers as I could, both on television and, when possible, live. At Christmas I would use much of the money given by friends and family to buy the scripts of comedy shows. I particularly enjoyed *The Goons*, *Morecambe and Wise* and *The Two Ronnies*. I would pore over their gags and then I would have a go at writing my own. I have to say that the first few scripts I wrote were absolute rubbish! They were rewrites of all the material I had heard, read or seen. Some of them would start off as *Morecambe and Wise* and finish as *The Two Ronnies*!

While I was immersing myself in all this comedic writing, I decided that I wanted tap dancing lessons, because I had read somewhere that Morecambe and Wise had had them. Right through my life my parents have been fantastically supportive of everything I've attempted. I think my request for tap dancing lessons was one step too far for Dad.

Those early shows on Mumbles Pier were a mixture of outdoor and party games plus general clowning. I would balance water on my head and then drop it so that the water would pour down my trousers. It was a typical Eighties holiday camp show. We would ask people to the front to try and shave a balloon without popping it. There would be Hoola Hoop competitions and lots of other activities, plus games to involve the whole family. Without a doubt those Pier Shows were the most traditional I ever did before I progressed to incorporate more home-spun comedy and magic.

They did, however, lead to more bookings. Brian asked me to do some beach club shows on The Slip in Mumbles and some shows in community centres. People who had seen me perform started booking me to do children's parties. I was then asked to accompany Dave Pope, a gospel singer, and I toured all over Britain for a few weeks working as the Technical Director. When I returned to Swansea, the Easter season was upon us and I started doing more open air gigs for Brian.

At the end of that summer (1982), I returned to theological college, only this time it was Elim College in Capel, Surrey. During the summer vacations I would run family shows at the Patti Pavilion, perform at the beach clubs and be involved in summer play schemes and commercial events like the Welsh Boat Show.

On leaving Elim College, I resolved to use my clowning work to try and bring children into the Church. Many of the churches connected with the college booked me. The work took me far and wide, and I got to visit many new places, such as the Channel Islands, Ireland and Belgium. I didn't have any language difficulties, as the churches I worked with were English-speaking. I did, however, encounter quite a lot of cultural problems, as many of the places in which I worked were not used to my style and they found it difficult to approve my work. In West Wales and Scotland there were difficult moments when members of the congregation said they disapproved of what I did.

Despite the negativity that many people feel towards clowning, it got me established, it paid my bills and I suppose it got me known as a personality in the entertainment world. It also gave me the opportunity to bring some light and happiness to many sad and deprived areas of the United Kingdom. Because I was funded by the Church and other religious organisations, I believe I was able to take shows to areas and schools that wouldn't normally be able to afford live theatre.

On one occasion, my wife, Rosie, and I were on our way to a friend's wedding in Scotland when I rang home to talk to my mother who was house-sitting for us. She told me that I had received a phone call from an agent who wanted me to do some children's entertainment at the home of the Duke and Duchess of Westminster, near Chester. The fee I was being offered was higher than anything I had been given in the past. That phone call was to take my performances into new realms.

When Rosie and I drove down their drive, I turned

to her and said, "We need a service station. I'm going to have to refuel if I'm to get to the end of this drive." I have never seen such a huge approach to anyone's house. It also reminded me that the last time I had worked in Chester I had been in the notorious Lache Estate. The area was terribly deprived and I will never forget that on one of the streets in a council estate there was a huge hole in the middle of the road. It filled up with water and the children, who were dressed in bathers, were jumping into the hole and using it as a paddling pool.

As we approached their baronial home, it was difficult to believe we were so close to the poverty we had encountered the other side of the city. In spite of the stark differences, the Duke and Duchess had a great charitable spirit and were very good to the people in the area. When we arrived we were confronted with two properties. One looked like a typical stately home, while the other was more modern and looked like an office block. A fellow was coming out holding balloons. I explained why we were there, and motioning towards the main house, he said, "There's a guy in there who will sort you out." I went in and saw a man in a tatty jumper and a pair of black jeans watching black and white television. Assuming he was a chauffeur or the handyman, I said, "I've come to do the party." He replied, "My wife's dealing with that," and continued to watch television. I noticed two women walking down the stairs. One was elderly and the other was young. I decided that the younger of the two was probably the chauffeur's wife, and putting on my best Swansea accent to make her feel at home, I said,

"All right, luv? We've come to do the party for the kids." I could see through the corner of my eye that the old lady's face was covered with one of the most horrified looks I have ever seen. She pointed to the younger woman and then looking pointedly at me, said, "This is her Grace!" I had obviously just called the Duchess 'luv', and relegated the Duke to the role of a chauffeur.

I did the show, surrounded by private photographs of the Queen – the type of pictures all of us would have in our family albums. It was slightly surreal to see so many happy snaps of the Queen building sand castles and playing with her children.

A few weeks later I did a Tear Fund tour which took me to London for one week and Manchester for another. Within a few days, I was being exposed to the great extremes of life in Britain. At that time, the Duke of Westminster was the wealthiest man in the United Kingdom. The area of Manchester where I was working was considered to be the poorest area in the North West of England. I did exactly the same act for Manchester and the children clapped, laughed and cheered at the same places as the more privileged children in the Duke's residence.

That experience helped me realise that children are children wherever you find them, and it made me resolve that I wanted them to fulfil their full potential. Every child in this country should have the right to realise their dreams. They should be helped to rise as far and as high as they can possibly go, so that when they are older and review their lives, they can console themselves that they had a go, rather than look back on a catalogue of regrets.

The 'Cheshire Set' were very kind to us as a family. By then I was a minister in Garston earning as little as £9 a week. Many Christians would tell me that The Lord would provide, but I found that Asda wouldn't accept that as a payment. I often found that God's provision would come in the form of an unexpected gig.

Because I had done a party at the home of the Duke and Duchess of Westminster, word spread through the stately homes of Cheshire and I ended up doing the entertainment at children's parties in most of them. Rosie would accompany me so that she could do the puppetry, and we would also take our baby son, Owain. In all the houses where we performed we would be asked to join the family for food, so that Owain has the distinction of being wined and dined (or at least dined) in almost all the great houses of Cheshire.

When these families phoned to make a booking they would say, "How much do you charge?" As soon as I heard that question, I would play for time.

"It depends," I'd reply. "Are you rich, super rich or mega rich?" Mercifully they would always reply, "We're super rich."

After one show, the father came to me and said, "I know what you normally charge, Kevin, but you've travelled a little further for this one, so I've signed a cheque but I've left the amount blank. Just write what you would like." I walked away from that gig with £150, which was a huge amount for us as a family. We ate very well that week.

I enjoyed working in the stately homes as much as the poorer areas of Britain. To me people are people, whatever their background. I have the same respect for the poorest as for the richest. While that belief comes partly from my faith, it comes also from my genuine love for people and the excitement I feel when I meet new individuals. My big passion in life is people.

Entertaining children as part of my work for the Relief Agency, Tear Fund, brought me into contact with youngsters from a very different background from those I encountered in the stately homes. The organisation wanted me to do one big show with a drama company called Primary Colours and the singer Ben Okafor. Normally we would work for a week and then finish with one big show. We had done this in London and Manchester. On this occasion they planned an event at the Civic Hall in Motherwell, but unfortunately, the budget wouldn't stretch far enough for all of us to work for the week before the concert.

However, I had lots of contacts in Scotland – due to my previous visits and the fact that Rosie originates from Greenock – and I was invited to work in Kirkintilloch and Dumbarton. There, I encountered poverty and tough situations, the like of which I had never seen before. There were two girls, who because of problems in the family, found that they never had enough food to eat in their house. They would go into shops and shoplift in a unique way. They never took the food outside the premises; they were so ravenous they would just sit on the floor and eat the food in the store.

There were two other children whose parents had chronic alcohol problems and never had enough money to buy food for them. The children were forced to go knocking on doors, asking for any empty bottles, because in those days you could get money from the shops for returning the empties.

For my children's shows, I used to buy several huge bags of balloons and keep them in a large props box. Someone stole all my balloons. I was furious because I still had nearly a week's entertainment ahead of me in Scotland and then I was going on to York for a week. I needed those balloons. Someone said to me they knew who pinched them and it turned out to be the two little girls. I thought, well, if they get a little happiness from those balloons, so be it. It won't cost me much to nip into Glasgow and buy some more.

In the past few years, I have been doing serious theatre work with Wales Theatre Company and Fluellen, so I tend not to talk much about the children's entertainment side of my career. But when you look back and think about the joy you brought to children and adults, you start to see it from a totally different perspective.

For example, I once worked for a week on the Isle of Guernsey. When you go there, even as a clown, you soon become a celebrity, because not a lot of entertainers visit the island. At the end of my week, a man came to me and said, "Do you know by the Tuesday (I'd started there on the Monday) I was really fed up with you. For two days my children came home and talked about nothing except this fabulous clown they had seen in school. Driving to work on the Wednesday, I put on the car radio and your name was mentioned almost straight away. On Thursday night, I sat down to watch Channel News and you were being interviewed. I opened the paper on Friday and there was a big article about you. The worst thing was that the same day, my children came home from the Kids' Club and said I had to go to the church with them on Sunday, because you were doing a Family Service."

That Sunday became a life-changing day for him. Unknown to the husband, his wife was on the brink of asking him to leave because he had a severe gambling problem which was putting a huge strain on her and the rest of the family. Following that service, he managed to turn things around and overcome his addiction. I like to think that it happened because I went to Guernsey in a colourful suit and a red nose.

As well as bringing me into contact with adults and children who have severe social problems, my children's entertaining has also taken me into some very bizarre situations. I worked in clubs and community halls in the Rhondda. There was a group in Porth who collected Easter eggs for distribution to needy and disabled children in the area. Porth Rugby Club organised an event and invited children to come and enjoy the entertainment and receive their chocolate presents. The three main acts that day were Stan Stennett, Bonnie Tyler and me. I suddenly realised it was turning into one of the most surreal moments of my life. There I was, standing on stage with Stan and Bonnie, singing children's songs.

Stan turned to me and said, "What shall we sing, Kev?"

So I answered, imitating Bonnie's voice, "I was loooorst in France." She turned to me and said, away from the hearing of the children, "Listen here, you cheeky bugger, it's not 'I Was Lost in France' that I was husky on, but 'It's A Heartache'!" Lots of people will have different views about Bonnie Tyler. My lasting memory is seeing her sitting there in Porth Rugby Club with a disabled child on her lap, wiping food away from his mouth as he struggled to eat.

I started this chapter expressing concerns about being dubbed a clown. I end it by saying I am not ashamed of that experience. I feel privileged to have met so many wonderful people, both young and old. I also accept that the community centres, stately homes, sea side slip and the huge concert halls were all a great preparation for my future – a future in which pantomime was to play a huge part.

CHAPTER 3

Behind You!

MY LOVE FOR PANTOMIME started long before I applied the grease paint and strutted my stuff on the boards at Port Talbot, Porthcawl and Swansea's Grand Theatre. As a boy in the Sixties, I was taken to see the pantomime at the Grand. In those days, the principal boys and principal girls tended to be played by pop stars. The only one I saw outside Swansea was at the Bristol Hippodrome with Larry Grayson and Rod Hull and Emu. I thought they were absolutely fantastic, and in my first variety show as a teenager, I did an act with an emu which my father bought me. I was captivated by this idea of an entertainer working with an animal puppet and I progressed from an emu to stuffing my hand up the back of a Fozzie Bear!

Despite being hooked as a youngster by Grayson and Hull, for me the absolute master of entertainment was Ryan Davies, who was a member of the famous Welsh comedy duo, Ronnie and Ryan. When I was a teenager, I went to see them perform. At that time I knew that I wanted to be an entertainer for the rest of my life. Ryan Davies was the greatest performer in the history of Welsh entertainment. No one could do what he could. He could play the piano at the level of a concert pianist, sing and act. He influenced me greatly in the sense that I wanted to be him. I wanted to hear the applause he heard.

I was six when I saw my first pantomime. I find it difficult to believe that I now perform on the stage that filled me with such excitement as a little boy. As a professional performer, I often go backstage in the Swansea Grand Theatre and have a sneaky look at all the old posters and think to myself, I saw that show. Little did I know then that, forty years on, I would be a performer rather than a member of the audience.

Paul Daniels used to end his show by walking from one side of the stage to the other and saying to the audience, "Just bear with me for a moment, ladies and gentlemen. Look at the size of this stage. Now go home and compare it with your television and decide which is the bigger." There is no comparison and that's why I think pantomime is such an important art form.

We have a chance to hook children with a show that has music, dancing, comedy, magic and special effects, so that they will come back when they are older to see other aspects of live theatre. Pantomime is growing an audience of people who may take to the stage at the National Theatre or fill our auditoriums as audiences. As I watched those pantomimes when I was a youngster, I wanted to be the characters I saw.

Pantomime has gripped me so strongly throughout my life that I spent part of my honeymoon watching Anna Neagle, Paul Nicholson and Des O'Connor in pantomime at the London Palladium. That was one of the big treats of our honeymoon, in addition to a trip to the House of Commons!

The first pantomime in which I acted was in 1992 at the Grand Pavilion, Porthcawl. I'd done a couple of summer seasons there as a children's entertainer, and Roger Pryce, who was the Entertainments Officer at Ogwr Council, was keen to get me started as a professional performer. He asked me to play Wishee-Washee in *Aladdin*. It ran for four weeks and gave me my first big chance on the professional stage.

Frank Hennessy was booked to play Abanazer but was taken ill before rehearsals. William Boyde, who played a nasty piece of work in *EastEnders* called James Wilmott-Brown, stood in for Frank. He'd never done pantomime before, only serious acting, and he was very nervous. He went to Norman Robbins who was the Dame and directing the show.

"Norman," he said, "When I come on, how will the children know that I'm the baddy? Everyone else gets an introduction. How will they know?" Norman replied, "Well, they'll just know." William was still not convinced.

"But," he persisted, "we'll have to do something."

Following the dress rehearsal, we did a performance to a very small audience of children who had been invited by local councillors. The children came mainly from disadvantaged areas and had all experienced tough upbringings. The curtains went up, the overture started and Abanazer walked out to some very dramatic chords. The children began to boo, hiss and throw sweets at him. I'm sure their response owed a lot more to their harsh backgrounds than Abanazer's appearance or his entrance. The actor came off stage into the wings, and smiling from head to toe, said, "They knew. They knew!" That was my first experience of pantomime, and I had four wonderful years at Porthcawl.

In the second year, I played one of the Ugly Sisters in *Cinderella*, and the following year I was asked to top the bill in *Jack and the Beanstalk*, which I considered a great honour.

In 1995 it looked as though I would be leaving Porthcawl to act in a pantomime at the Swansea Grand Theatre, as I'd been invited to play the King in *Jack and the Beanstalk*. This was what I had been working towards, and for me it would be the pinnacle of my career to date. Then I discovered that Sophie Lawrence and Steve Lewis would be playing Porthcawl. I was a huge fan of Sophie, and the thought of standing on the same stage with her and getting paid for it was too great an opportunity to miss. I rang the Pavilion at Porthcawl and said, "Look, I know I said I wouldn't be with you this year, but if there's still some money in the pot, I would love to change my mind and appear with Sophie and Steven in *Babes in the Wood*." They were happy for me to return, so I played the Good Robber which was to be my last performance in pantomime at Porthcawl.

By a strange quirk of fate, I was to appear in the same show for my first pantomime at the Swansea Grand. However, the forces of political correctness insisted that it should be called *Robin Hood*, as it was no longer acceptable to kidnap children and take them into the forest. It is, though, quite all right to be an outlaw!

Unfortunately, it was something of a disappointment for me. We had a huge cast with class actors such as Little and Large and Ruth Madoc. There were just too many people in the cast. It was really difficult for us all to gel, and it turned out to be an unhappy show with the inevitable personality clashes. So, whilst my first appearance in pantomime at the Grand was something I had looked forward to for years, it was filled with difficulties.

Nowadays, I am known as a pantomime dame, but interestingly, my first seven performances involved me playing all kinds of characters. I played one of the Merry Men in my first appearance at the Grand, and then in the *Millennium Pantomime* at the same theatre I played the Emperor of China, for which I received excellent reviews. Of all the reviews, I will never forget one which appeared in a magazine devoted mainly to amateur dramatics. It was written by a very grand lady who used the language of Middle England. She said in her article, "I do not know who was playing the part of the Emperor of China, but he must have been very popular, because everyone cheered whenever he came on. However, the way he spoke was more like a Welsh potter than the Emperor of China." Ever since that review I have tried to fathom how Welsh potters speak, but I still don't know.

At the end of that performance, Paul Elliot, who was part of the newly-formed production company, QDOS, knocked on my door and said, "Dame next year." True to his word, he booked me for the next pantomime, and I played my first pantomime dame in *Snow White and the*

Seven Dwarfs. I will never forget that production, not just because it was the fulfilment of a long-held dream to play the Dame, but also because I teamed up with Mike Doyle. I first met Mike when I was responsible for the entertainment at his child's birthday party at his home in Newport. With Mike, I have built up an almost mystical relationship on stage. We only have to look at each other and the other will know what to do. It's almost like playing sport. If I'm floundering, I pass the ball to Mike and he will sort it out. I believe it works the same way for him, too. It very rarely happens, but if we have to carry each other, then we will. Of all the pantomimes I have done, the ones I have done with Mike have been the most enjoyable.

As well as playing with Mike, I have been privileged to act opposite many famous actors. Whilst the posters and fliers would say that they are the stars of the show, I have been in many productions when the children from the audience have stolen the limelight. The section of the pantomime where the audience sing from the song sheet and children come onto the stage is always a highlight for me. I am thrilled that it is still an integral part of the show at the Swansea Grand Theatre. Many venues throughout Britain, because of the current health and safety laws, have stopped the children's input. There are fears that the child may fall onto or off the stage and some theatres are even afraid of throwing out sweets in case a bonbon ruptures a child's retina.

On many occasions I have been in full flow, extemporising with some of the children, making the audience laugh, when one of the quieter youngsters will tug at the sleeve of my costume. And then I hear those immortal words uttered throughout the land and feared by all pantomime actors, "I want a pee." You try to concentrate on the others but the statements, "I want a pee. I want to go to the toilet," become more and more insistent.

The persistence of children and their refusal to accept your answers is what makes this spot so funny for the audience and so nerve-wracking for the actors. Time and time again when I am dressed as the Dame, I will be aware of one of the children staring at me throughout the banter. Then he will say, "You're a man, aren't you?"

"Yes," I reply, thinking that's the end of the matter, but of course it never is. Still looking at me, he will point to one of the other actors and say, "Well, how come you are his mother then?"

Of course, it's not just the children who come out with the funny lines. Sometimes their presence gives the actor a chance to land a funny. In one pantomime, soon after Swansea City had started sharing the Liberty Stadium with the Ospreys rugby team, a girl came on to the stage wearing an Ospreys' shirt. I heard that the Ospreys were being hammered by the Cardiff Blues. Being an ardent football fan, I couldn't resist the opportunity for a quick gibe.

"So you're an Ospreys fan?" I asked.

"Yes," she replied.

"We've just had a phone call from someone who's at the match," I said, "and he saw one of his friends at the game and said to him, 'I'm surprised you're here tonight. I thought you'd be at the panto.' His friend replied, 'I am at the panto. I'm watching the Ospreys!'"

As a football fan, my one regret about the new Liberty Stadium is that it is so far away from the theatre. When the Swans played at the Vetch, with careful timing during a Saturday matinee, I could always see the last twenty-five minutes of the football. Everyone in the theatre would know that the Swans were playing at home, because my song sheet would be considerably shorter, and when the curtain came down I would be off that stage running faster than anyone had ever managed in the history of six-inch heels.

When I was in *Cinderella* playing the Ugly Sister, I had the greatest difficulty. The heels were the highest I'd ever seen, so that slowed me down, and the costumes were so voluminous, it took me forever to change back into civvies. The make-up was also the most outrageous I'd ever used. Not using grease paint, I found the cheap and tarty lip stick I'd applied was very hard to wash off. I slipped my trousers over my tights, gave my face one quick wipe and legged it across the dual carriageway to see the Swans. The stewards always knew I'd be coming, so they would open the gates to let me in. People in the stand would turn to me and say, "You've still got your make-up on, Kev!" My son and father who always kept me a seat would be cowering next to me, mortified with embarrassment. The greatest twenty-five minutes I ever saw was when I witnessed three goals and three sending-offs, so that was definitely worth the embarrassment!

The one Saturday matinee I will never forget had nothing

at all to do with football. There are often long hold-ups to accommodate large coach parties and Saturday afternoon performances sometimes start later than scheduled. In this particular show we were doing *Goldilocks and the Three Bears*. Waiting for clearance, five minutes soon became ten minutes which eventually became twenty. From the wings, we could tell that the audience were growing restless. At first we were informed that a gentleman who had come with his wife and granddaughter had been taken ill in the Upper Circle. A little later we were given the devastating news that he had died. We knew that we had to do something and I suppose, in the tradition of circus, the management decided to send in the clowns. Danny Adams, Clive Webb, Lisa Riley and I, plus a couple of other characters, went into the audience with balloons and sweets, and we tried to work the stalls and the lower circle as best we could, because people in those sections of the auditorium didn't know what had happened. We were aware that we had to keep the children occupied. We said there had been one or two technical difficulties, but throughout the afternoon news of what had actually happened spread around the auditorium. As members of the cast, we had a collection to buy a bouquet for the widow, and every cast member signed a card expressing our sorrow at her terrible loss.

When Lisa Riley appeared at the Grand, she was well known through her appearances on *Emmerdale* and *You've Been Framed*. Lisa is an extremely talented actress who holds the company together and she has become a close family friend. Many people link her with the Mandy Dingle character in *Emmerdale*, but she has also proved her acting ability with great performances in TV shows such as *Fat Friends*. In one episode of *The Bill* she played the part of a bullied cinema worker and again proved her acting prowess with a superb performance.

She has shown that she can act on television and the stage, whereas many actors can't do both. Lisa is also one of those large people, who, like me (I hope!), dispel the myth that large actors and actresses cannot move well on stage. In *Goldilocks and the Three Bears* she did the splits twice daily for thirty days and managed to get up every time!

When we were together on my radio show, we couldn't stop laughing. She brought several members of the dancing troupe with her. They were all affectionately known in the studio as 'Kev's Bitches'. That year, playing *Goldilocks and the Three Bears*, we had great fun, and my one memory of the experience is that there seemed to be constant laughter around the place.

In the cast we had a comedy duo called Clive Webb and Danny Adams. Clive used to be on the TV show, *Tiswas*, and Danny is one of those multi-talented comedians who can use a unicycle, dance, sing and act. In pantomime at the Grand, there is a tradition for members of the cast to play games such as Murder. You go around and shoot whoever you think is the murderer, but you can't just say, "You're dead!" You have to make some kind of noise that imitates a gun. Not content with saying "bang" or using a cheap cap gun like the rest of us, Clive bought a starting pistol and frightened the living daylights out of everyone backstage. He and Danny added to the general feeling of fun and happiness and helped to make that show truly memorable.

Danny, Clive and Lisa Riley were great to act with, and one of the joys of working in pantomime has been the many wonderful characters I have met. When I worked with Dora Bryan she was in her eighties and yet she seemed to have far more energy than the rest of the cast. On the night the run ended, there was a party, but Dora must have left the theatre about 9.30 p.m. and gone back to her room at the Marriott Hotel. She said she needed an early night so she could catch the six o'clock morning train to London, where she was starting rehearsals for a new show at ten o'clock!

A wonderful story is told about her. We modern actors leave theatres by the quickest route, which tends to be through the main entrance. Dora, being a consummate professional of the old school, would only ever enter or leave theatres by the stage door. She was performing in a particular place, and of course, she had only ever seen the theatre through the stage door entrance at the rear of the building. One day she decided to go for a walk through the town, and stumbled across a very interesting-looking theatre. She went through the main doors and asked the girl on reception whether they had a matinee show that afternoon. She looked at Dora and said, "Yes... and you're in it!"

One of the great things about working in pantomime is that you get drawn into a real group of like-minded friends and hear fabulous stories about household names. Norman Robbins, with whom I'd acted at Porthcawl, had met and worked with Jimmy Jewell and Hilda Baker. Like many successful double acts in theatre, they didn't particularly like each other. In Blackpool they were doing a live version of their TV show, *Nearest and Dearest*. They argued about whose name should go first on the large hoardings outside the theatre. Should it be Jimmy Jewell and Hilda Baker or Hilda Baker and Jimmy Jewell? Finally they came to an agreement that they would change the names around each week. Norman came out of the building one morning and was aware of a huge commotion. He saw a young chorus boy holding a ladder. Halfway up, with dress akimbo and flapping knickers, was Hilda Baker, measuring the letters to make sure that her name was the same size as that of Jimmy Jewell!

As someone who grew up in the Sixties watching situation comedies on television, I sometimes have to pinch myself when I realise I am on stage with an actor who played Blakey in *On The Buses* or someone like John Challis who played Boycie in *Only Fools and Horses*. I worked with John Challis on *Peter Pan*. Jenna Lee Jones, who has since played Scaramouche in *We Will Rock You* in the West End, was playing *Peter Pan*. John Challis was such a good actor that he made Captain Hook look and sound almost Shakespearean.

There was a wonderful scene where Peter Pan flew across the auditorium. John would stand on stage riling Pan, shouting, "Come on, Pan, come and get me." Mike Doyle and I were playing Captain Hook's sidekicks, Starkey and Smee. One night while we were on stage, Jenna started her flight across the auditorium but got stuck halfway across. Hanging above the audience, she was technically perfectly safe but internally she must have been terrified. John broke into an ad-libbed soliloquy, imploring Pan not to hang there for too long, but to come and face the music. He was so convincing, I'm sure the audience thought the whole incident was part of the production!

I also thoroughly enjoyed playing opposite Vicki Michelle in the 1999-2000 production of *Aladdin*. She played the Genie and I played the Emperor. We fooled around most of the time and I suppose we were regarded as the two pranksters in the company. On one occasion we put Andy Linford's underpants in the freezer compartment of the fridge, without realising that they were the only underpants he had with him that night. He had to put them on. They were freezing. I've never seen any one leave the theatre with such a strange walk.

On another occasion, I managed to convince one of the staff at Swansea Sound to phone up Vicki and pretend he was doing an interview for hospital radio. On purpose he got absolutely everything wrong. He pretended that he thought she was the character with the blonde hair in *Allo Allo*, and he asked her how was panto with Jim Vincent, instead of Tim Vincent. We managed to obtain a copy of the interview, and when she heard it, she realised that it was shot through with mistakes. Eventually, she accepted it was a send-up, and fortunately, took it all in good humour, as it was the kind of prank she would happily play on someone else.

After one of the shows, a reader wrote to the *Swansea Evening Post* and said that I was one of his top four comedy performers. The other three were Vicki, Melvyn Hayes and Joe Pasquale. He was pleading with the powers that be to give him his dream show and put the four of us in one pantomime. I've never acted with Melvyn Hayes but I have interviewed him for the radio and I was excited by the fact that he was even smaller than me. What came across though was his fitness and amazing energy. I grew up watching him in the Cliff Richard films and *It Ain't Half Hot Mum*. For me, that was one of the great British ensemble comedy pieces. You didn't have one big name; the whole cast were the stars.

Joe Pasquale and I have never done pantomime together, although we have done a number of charity shows. I would like to play Dame to Joe's comic, but I'd have a few problems with Melvyn, as he would also want to play the Dame. Perhaps we could manage the Ugly Sisters together, and of course, I would jump at the chance of playing opposite Vicki Michelle again. Vicki is a joy to work with. She is a wonderful company player. That is one of the greatest things anyone has ever said about my acting. Peter Karrie claimed that I was a company man and great to have in the team. Sadly, some actors play for themselves, rather than for the rest of the cast.

Just as the reader of the newspaper fantasised about my fellow actors, I have often thought of others who I'd like to act with. I would love to play Smee to Leslie Grantham's Captain Hook in *Peter Pan*. Many people cannot see beyond Dirty Den when they think of him, but for me he is a first class actor and lovely person. Or, if he wasn't up for that, I could play Widow Twanky to his Abanazer.

Claire Sweeney is someone else with whom I'd like to work. She is a good pantomime performer. That would be an important point for me; not just to work with people who are good straight actors, but I want them to know the rudiments of good pantomime which I believe is a specialist genre. Leslie Grantham certainly understands that, as does Claire. They're not luvvies trying to play to the balcony, but solid performers who know how to get the job done.

I have been fortunate to meet and act with so many great people. Pantomime has given me so much, and in my own way, I have tried to pay it back. A friend of mine in London rang me a couple of years ago and said, "What are you doing in the *Guardian* dressed as a Dame?" Often at lunchtime, in full costume, I would pop into the Brunswick Church Luncheon Club for elderly people. The other members of staff were also dressed in pantomime costumes, and it just so happened that this particular day the *Guardian* was covering the story that Help the Aged were fighting to keep the facility going. I was pleased to add my weight to the campaign, as I read that in one year over thirty elderly people in Wales had died of starvation.

It has also been a tradition at the Grand that either just before or after Christmas members of the cast will visit the children's wards in the local hospitals. The children enjoy our visits but often I think the nurses are even more excited, especially when I turn up with a good-looking lad like Gary Beadle.

During the 2006–7 production of *Dick Whittington*, I

took several of the dancers with me. One fifteen-year-old boy was recovering from an operation and was asleep when we entered his ward. His father was devastated on his son's behalf that he had missed this bevvy of beautiful girls. They lined up around his bed leaning forward as if they were going to kiss him. The father took a photo so that he could show him what he had missed while he was asleep!

These visits are nothing to do with PR exercises or photo shoots, and in fact in the past few years we have gone into the hospitals without a cameraman. We are there because we want to be there and because we care.

I love playing pantomime but of course there are many other things I enjoy. In fact, I sometimes think it would have been easier to have been around forty years ago. In those days, people didn't mind if you crossed over the boundaries. Nowadays, people want to pigeonhole you. You must be one thing or the other. In fact one agent told me, "We're having trouble with you, Kev. We don't know what you are or where to place you. Are you a dame, a serious actor, a broadcaster, or what?"

Broadcasting has given me another major problem. I have loved playing the Dame at the Grand in Swansea. However, sometimes I think it would be good to try my hand in other theatres, but I can't because of my daily commitment to my early morning show on Swansea Sound. This dilemma was underlined for me when after *Snow White and the Seven Dwarfs*, Lisa Riley and most of the cast went to Sunderland the following year. I received several texts from many of the actors saying, "It's not the same without you, Kev."

In spite of that, I love getting up at five o'clock in the morning to go and meet my listening public at six. Honest! Just like pantomime, the radio has given me a huge amount of fun and some amazing memories.

Handsome Boy! Baby Kev. I was 12 months old and the photo was displayed in the photographer's window in Woodfield St, Morriston. What can't be seen is my dad, holding me still through a gap in the chair.

As a toddler outside our first family home in Bartley Terrace, Plasmarl.

'Where's Kev?' Plasmarl Junior School.

One of the scariest moments of my life (and a bad hair day). Minutes after this picture was taken I had to hop at sea from the pilot boat on to the navy ship in the backgound for a broadcast.

Just before take off! Flying gliders with the Air Cadets.

I love dogs and even
on my Graduation
Day I find a puppy
for a picture.

Above: With lovely Marilyn Harry, George Miller and Kevin Tugwell when I was part of the Elim Church Evangelistic Team.

Below: At a Charity Ball with the lovely Joan Collins and Swansea writer Alex Frith, who has always been very supportive to me and the family.

A terrible picture – but happy memories of the first church that I was pastor of in Garston. We shared the building with the Welsh Chapel of Liverpool.

Mike Doyle and I during a dress rehearsal for *Snow White,* our first panto together. Mike takes this picture with him and puts it up in his panto dressing room wherever he works.

Handsome Man!
Dame Trot!

As Buttons in
Cinderella in
Porthcawl.

Above: Paula Frances played Cinders. I don't know why I'm looking so scared – we were celebrating a sell-out!

Left: I loved my time in Porthcawl, and *Jack and the Beanstalk* gave me my first chance to top the bill with my sidekick, Dewi the Dragon.

Above: With all the dads of Kingsbridge Colts, before a
game in Loyat in France on a twinning tour. My good mate
Brian Griffiths is on the back row with a teenage-looking
moustache! I scored the winning goal!

Below: Swansea Sound Allstars. With the charity football
team before a fundraising game. I'm in the front row, next to
Sianey – well, I'm captain. My son Owain is in the back row
next to Steve in the white shirt. No, not the one with the
chain – he's the mayor, mun!

Above: Launching a Swansea Bay Stroll with the *Evening Post*.

Below: With a film crew at the Vetch during a Channel Four programme on Kev's Swansea with Monty Don.

A very rare photo of me in Clown's Motley during the filming of a *Highway* Christmas Special with dear Harry Secombe.

A happy family at one of our favourite holiday destinations – Disneyland, Paris. Rosie is smiling as she takes a picture of Owain, Bethan and me outside It's a Small World.

Above: The Big Day! Rosie and I at our wedding in Colwyn Bay in 1986.

Below: A panto party to remember! Now where is that poison apple? Celebrating the end of a successful panto run with the lovely Gillian Taylforth and one of the nicest of performers in Theatre, Fogwell Flax.

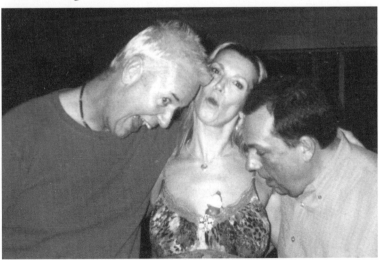

Above: Me! More pretty girls! The Emperor of China!

Below: With two very talented young performers: Welsh actress Rochelle, who played Snow White, and my really good friend Nicky, who taught me all I know about dancing.

Above: The Greatest Crew in all the earth. Another party with the fantastic Grand Theatre crew.

Below: No, you're not seeing things! Interviewing Marilyn Monroe at Universal Studios, Florida.

Above: It gets even more bizarre! This time I'm interviewing Beetlejuice.

Left: In Plasmarl with my dear gran, Gertie Thomas – known as Mam Thomas.

Above: My other gran, known as Nan – Iris from the 'Afod.

Right: You can't go in the fountain! Owain with Dad in Florida.

Not quite Gene Kelly…

Early days. I played Jacob in *Joseph and his Amazing Technicolour Dreamcoat* at Dynever School. These are some of my wives! I had a real soft spot for one of the three – but it's my secret!

CHAPTER 4

Kev Calling

FROM AN EARLY AGE I have been drawn by the magic of radio. In the days when local radio was more community-based than it is now, I appeared on several Swansea Sound programmes. While I was at the London Bible College, my interest broadened as I became involved with some religious broadcasting on LBC Radio in London. Laurence Spicer, who was vastly experienced and highly regarded in the world of radio, asked me to write and present some *Thought for the Week* programmes. I was so excited by the possibilities that I put a demo tape together and applied for a place in the National School of Broadcasting. It was tastily located in Soho with a strip joint on one side and a massage parlour the other. I was accepted, but unfortunately, the fees were too high. As a family we couldn't find the money and I was unable to secure sponsorship.

I have to admit that for a long time after that disappointment I believed that radio would never happen for me. When I moved back to Swansea in the late Eighties, I tried to break into it once again. This time I sent several ideas for series of programmes to Swansea Sound, but never received a reply.

Then one day, I happened to be doing an interview for

BBC Radio Wales during which I slipped into one of my entertaining stories about my life (at least I hope they're entertaining). At the end of the piece, the interviewer told me he'd enjoyed the story and asked whether I'd ever thought of working on radio. It was pretty obvious by my response that I had, so he took me to meet his producer, Paul Evans, who in those days was based in the Swansea studio.

From that chance meeting I was given a series on BBC Radio Wales. It was called *Child's Play* and the idea behind the programmes was that I would interview children on a certain topic and then talk to people over sixty on the same theme. We would talk to the children about issues such as Sports Days, shopping and education and then record the memories of older people. The programmes would show how attitudes had changed over the decades and the series became very popular. On the first programme which was about Sports Days in schools, I had the great joy of interviewing my grandmother.

The other joy about the six-programme series was that it was always repeated on the *Best of Wales*, so I would receive a repeat fee. After the last programme, they decided to repeat the entire series the following year, so I got yet another repeat fee. I was beginning to realise that this was the life for me: one job, three wages!

I made a one-off programme called *A Christmas in Wales* which followed a similar format in that we recorded children preparing for Christmas in their schools, and again we interviewed older people for their memories of the festive season in the Thirties, Forties and Fifties. Five Live, or Radio Five as it was called in those days, bought the programme and renamed it *Every Child's Christmas in Wales*. When I received their fee, I noticed the huge discrepancies in payment between national and commercial radio.

After this flurry of broadcasting activity – which also included a one-off music programme – everything went quiet again, as often happens in the media. So I went back to Swansea Sound, and on the strength of my successes on Radio Wales, they booked me to present a children's show every Saturday morning. In turn, this led to them asking me to present a series called *Heart and Soul*, a Christian music programme, which I still present to this day. In 1993 the Programme Controller called me in and offered me the chance of presenting a daily show.

I know that some people find it difficult to speak on radio. They feel as if they're talking into 'The Great Void', but I have to admit that I have never had that problem. I always assume that I am talking to someone else. Once the red light comes on in the studio, it's no different from the fall spot picking me up on the stage. I enjoy the radio and I particularly like regional or local broadcasting because you are given the chance to interview people you know or know about.

When I bump into some of the Radio Wales broadcasters with whom I've worked in the past, people like Frank Hennessy, Roy Noble and Owen Money, they will say, "When are you coming back to join us?" I suppose the answer to that is, "No one's asked me!"

I have to admit that having lived in different parts of Wales,

I would like the opportunity to present the programmes I've done for Swansea Sound to a wider audience. I have received invitations to work for other radio companies. When Real Radio first came on air, they asked me to present their *Breakfast Show* and offered me a very attractive package. I decided not to leave Swansea Sound, so they then came back with a better offer but once again I decided to stay put. John Simons was the person who tried to woo me away to Real Radio, a station which broadcasts throughout the whole of South Wales. He was extremely encouraging and had several ideas about how he would help me develop my talent. I think John was quite upset that I turned the offer down.

I met John at the Vetch where he was watching his home team, Hartlepool, play the Swans. He said to me, "I think you just want to be a big fish in a small sea." I understood what he was saying, but I find it difficult to agree with the sentiment, because I don't consider myself a big fish. I'm just a local boy trying to make a living in his own area.

In addition, I don't regard the Swansea area as a small sea. I believe I'm living in a big ocean full of talent and potential. I still love working for Swansea Sound and I am privileged that, according to the statisticians, the station has one of the highest listenership figures in the UK for a Medium Wave station. I have a great loyalty to the station and many listeners have a loyalty to me.

It is dangerous to judge the popularity of a programme on the number of people who phone in. The *Sunday Hotline* is a chance for people to air their grievances about life in their own neighbourhood. Inevitably, the programme builds up a small clutch of people who are regular callers. Over the years I have talked to many great characters, such as Laurence Holmes, an ex-bin man who in his nineties was still telling the councillors in a most eloquent way that they were a load of rubbish. From conversations and chance meetings it is clear that we have a huge listening audience every Sunday and there are very few councillors or Assembly Members who don't listen each week.

Many radio stations struggle with the idea of programmes devoted to religious issues. Personally, I'm proud to present *Heart and Soul* which is devoted to gospel music. Such programmes are often only heard on Christian radio stations. The problem then is the danger of creating a Christian ghetto where such a programme is only heard by card-carrying Christians. The value of putting the programme on a commercial station is that you are increasing the audience, with people who would never find their way onto the frequency of a religious broadcaster.

As a genre, Christian music is just as interesting and professional as any other style. In addition, it reminds people that the gospel tradition is a major part of the history of music. The American and African forms have given us Christina Aguilera, Whitney Houston, Beyoncé and Leona Lewis. Some major performing concert artists such as Amy Grant have also come out of Christian music. I am glad that I am able to present this type of music on a major radio channel and not on some substation. The programme has the same audience potential as other programmes and I am pleased that the music is allowed to stand on its own.

On my *Breakfast with Kevin Johns* show I have editorial freedom. My sense of humour can sometimes land me into 'vatfulls' of hot water. On other occasions, I believe it helps. I see nothing wrong with poking mild fun at the Prime Minister and other leaders. I also believe that in the face of terrorism, humour is the only weapon I have. I have studied the broadcasting guidelines religiously and I know that there are times when I am very close to the limit, but so far I have never crossed the borderline of acceptability.

In addition to putting a humorous spin on serious issues, I also believe the programme can make a difference to people's lives. On one occasion, I was told to do an item on breast testing. In the excitement I completely misunderstood the directive and had images of measuring the vital statistics of Samantha Fox and other Page Three girls. Eventually, reality kicked in and I realised that I would be fronting a programme on medical issues.

As a husband, a father of a daughter, and someone whose grandmother had breast cancer, the programme taught me the importance of breast screening and early detection of the disease. After the week of interviews it was reported that there had been a significant increase in the number of women from the target audience who had come forward for tests. The hope is that every one of those tests was clear, but should something have been detected in time, then we can console ourselves that we did a good job.

One morning, hosting *The Hotline* in 2006, I was devastated to hear the number of elderly people in Wales who had died of starvation. On air, I told a man who worked as an elderly persons' campaigner, that if he could give me the names of two people who were in need of some help, I would give £100. By the end of the programme, the listeners had pledged a further £550 to feed vulnerable elderly people at Christmas.

It so happened that at the time these figures were being published, a major local story was the fact that the Salvation Army had been banned from playing carols in the Quadrant Shopping Centre. Market forces had led to Christmas stalls in the place where the band had traditionally played. Listeners were outraged by the development and the Salvation Army were also devastated, as they used the money raised to give elderly people meals at Christmas time. The money given by listeners was used to fill this gap, and the £100 which my wife, Rosie, and I donated was used to buy food parcels and presents for two elderly people who were particularly vulnerable. For me, this was local radio at its best, bringing help to the community as well as entertainment and easy listening.

The station has always tried to champion causes, and as an individual who has great sympathy for the rights of animals, I was happy to lend my weight to the campaign to stop the transportation of live veal. Much more popular as a dish in other countries, calves were being transported across Europe and often held and subsequently killed in appalling conditions. Across Britain, people gathered at airports to stop them being flown out. This resulted in the sellers trying to send the calves in aeroplanes from smaller privately-owned airfields.

News spread around the Swansea area that a Russian plane was being used on a regular basis to transfer the veal from Fairwood Airfield, Swansea. Our then Head of News, Lynne Courtney, was at Fairwood, linked to my programme. She was in the middle of an interview with a campaigner who had chained herself to the axle of one of the lorries carrying the veal. Over the distressing noise of the calves in the lorry, I suddenly heard other noises which alarmed me. Above the screams of other campaigners were the manic revving of a lorry's engine. The driver was ready to move, despite the fact that Lynne and the campaigner were underneath the vehicle trying to carry out an interview.

After that programme many people told me it was good radio. The campaigner and Lynne were safe, but of course the calves weren't. I found that live interview with Lynne one of the most harrowing I have ever done. She showed amazing bravery and incredible professionalism that day.

It is often the case that live broadcasting which captures the audience's imagination often deals with sad issues. That was certainly the case when Princess Diana was killed. The night before, I had been presenting a listener with a prize at one of the city's night clubs, so I hadn't arrived home until 1.00 a.m. I was to record *Heart and Soul* at 7.00 a.m. and I was also to stand in as presenter of the *Sunday Hotline* at 9.00 a.m.

At six o'clock I had a call from the station telling me the terrible news and asking me to get in as soon as possible. We turned the *Hotline* programme over to the listeners and asked them to phone in with their views on Diana. It was a very difficult programme to host. Although she was not a powerful figure in the royal line, it soon became clear from what people said, that in terms of people's feelings, she was the most important member of the Royal Family. Everyone talked about her as if she were a friend. There was a huge amount of grief on the airwaves that day.

I was on air in 1996 when Thomas Hamilton walked into Dunblane Primary School and killed several children and their teachers. When you see such news flash up on the screen in the studio, you know that you have to respond. As a father of young children, I had all kinds of emotions but I had to channel them into a professional response. That again was a very difficult programme, as was the day of Diana's funeral. By the time I came off air, I felt absolutely exhausted and drained.

Such incidents remind me that there is far more to the art of running radio programmes than spinning records and playing requests. Strangely, when I worked for Radio Wales, I was called a presenter, but when I joined Swansea Sound, I was called a DJ. I suppose I am not ashamed to carry that tag, but it doesn't capture the emotional grinder that I sometimes have to go through whilst presenting my shows. I have always thought of myself as a broadcaster rather than a DJ.

As an emotional being, I am not afraid of showing my feelings, and on a couple of occasions I've unashamedly cried during my broadcasts. Just before Christmas in 2006 on the *Sunday Hotline*, a gentleman rang the station. He was facing severe problems as his wife was disabled and his daughter was categorised as being Special Needs. His house was not adequately equipped to serve their needs. As a result of that interview, the Assembly Member, Peter Black, helped him, and his house was restructured to cope with disability issues.

Another listener contacted us to say that her daughter had severe behavioural problems and on occasion would smash up the house. As she told us her story, I found myself breaking down and crying on air. Sometimes you just have to go with the emotion of the moment and not be afraid to show the listeners that you are also human.

This sense of the station bringing the needs of individuals to a wider audience is an important aspect of the role of a broadcasting network. I lobbied the idea of The Local Heroes' Awards to Swansea Sound, which I had already done for our sister station, Valleys Radio.

In 2007, the Child of Courage Award was given to Nia, a young girl from Port Talbot who had a brain tumour. She came to the Awards event from a hospital in Cardiff. A local bridal dress shop had dressed her for her special evening and she looked radiant. We had been told that she was a huge Disney fan. After the singer Liz McClellend gave her the award, I came on and said to Nia, "I believe you love Disney." I then presented her with several Disney DVDs, video games and Disney princesses. Next I went into my pocket, pulled out an envelope and said, "Of course, the best way to see Cinderella is..." At that moment the audience gasped as they guessed what I was going to do next. I presented her with tickets for a trip to Disney World, Paris, on Eurostar.

The awards were made in April and the plan was that she and her family would take the trip in the summer when it was hoped she would be in better health. About ten days after the awards we had a phone call that left us in no doubt that if we wanted to get Nia to Paris we would have to send her soon, as the doctors felt she may only have three weeks to live. The doctors approved her trip. Ruth, who was one of our programme assistants at the time, arranged it through Travel House. My friend, Brian Griffiths, who has an airport taxi service was booked to transport Nia, her mother and grandmother to Waterloo Station where they would catch the Eurostar.

After we had made all the arrangements, we discovered that it was impossible to find any company to offer us insurance, as Nia was terminally ill. The insurers were nervous about the potentially great costs should she need medical care whilst on holiday. In the end, we had to break the dreadful news to her that we wouldn't be able to take her to Disney World. We were all devastated as Nia had set her heart on going.

Then, on her birthday, we received a phone call from an insurance company stating that they would help. As far as they were concerned, insurance companies had been set up in the first place to help people in such difficulties. The cover cost was about £500 and Swansea Sound paid for it. Ruth was able to go to Nia's house and gatecrash her birthday party with the news that like Cinderella, she would be going! They had a wonderful time in Paris.

A day after arriving back in Port Talbot, Nia took to her bed and died a week later. To this day her mother has wonderful memories of that trip and has set up a charity in honour of her daughter. For me there is no doubt that Nia was the bravest little girl I have ever met in my life.

The Local Heroes' Awards scheme has brought all kinds of unsung heroes to the public's attention. It has honoured a young, homeless man who dragged himself up from the streets to such an extent that he is now working full-time helping others. We have also been able to award prizes to people who have devoted their spare time to raising money for charities, and to young children who have become carers looking after sick parents.

On one occasion, I presented an award to a nurse who worked in her spare time as a volunteer on the Aberavon lifeboat. She was an angel twice over – on the wards and on the sea. These people are so important to our communities, and I feel privileged that I have been able to highlight their stories.

In addition to championing the cause of local people, much of my work in front of the mike involves interviewing the rich, the famous and the powerful. They don't come much more powerful than the Prime Minister, and I will never forget my Swansea Sound skirmish with Tony Blair during the first of my two interviews with him. I was asked to interview him at the Brangwyn Hall in Swansea after the Welsh Labour Party Conference. We were asked, or perhaps I should say told, to submit our questions well in advance. At this first interview, I had used up all my pre-submitted questions and we still had a couple of minutes to spare. I thought, he's a barrister, he's Prime Minister and he's Head of the Labour Party, so he's bound to enjoy an impromptu question. He'll surely love the sentiments behind my question.

Living in Gorseinon, I had seen the devastating effects on nearby Bryngwyn when the steel works had closed, making five hundred men redundant. I had also watched the workers march proudly down the streets on the Works' last day. I said, "One more question, Mr Blair." As I started my inquisition, I noticed that his many aides were looking decidedly uneasy.

"When you hear about major unemployment, those figures you hear on the news telling you that another five hundred jobs have gone, do you think to yourself that's just another statistic? Or do you see five hundred men who have to go home to their wives and families and say, 'It's not going to be such a good Christmas this year. We're going to have to increase the mortgage or I'm going to have to move to another part of the country to get a new job.' Or is it just another statistic?"

He pulled on his collar, coughed, went a little white and then gave me an answer about the global economy. He also claimed we would all like to stop the world and get off if we could, and then he returned to the global economy. I have to confess I was a little disappointed by that non-answer.

After the interview, I was sitting in the Green Room waiting for our sound engineer who was to give me a lift back to the radio station. Although located in Swansea, I definitely felt I was in Coventry, as no one was speaking to me because of my unscheduled question. Tony Blair was having a heated discussion with Neil Kinnock about some policy issue. Trying to sit quietly and unnoticed in the corner of the room, it was at that moment that my mobile phone went off. The ring tone was the Welsh National Anthem, and unfortunately, the longer it rang, the louder it became. I was wearing one of those coats you should never wear if you have to go to the toilet, as there are so many zips, you may open the wrong one. With every incorrect zip, *Hen Wlad Fy Nhadau* got louder and louder. I just could not find my mobile phone though I knew it was in one of the pockets. I was now definitely the centre of attention as Blair, Kinnock and the rest fell silent. When I eventually found my mobile, it was my father, saying, "Well done. I enjoyed that."

Kinnock then got up and moved towards me.

"Bloody hell! Where did you get that mobile phone ring from? Bloody marvellous tune that." As I was speaking to my father, I had to ask him to hold while I answered Neil Kinnock. Kinnock solved the problem by saying, "Give me the phone." He was now in direct contact with my dad. I could hear snatches of the conversation.

"It's Neil Kinnock, mun... How are you butt?... Well, very nice of you to say so, mun... I tell you, bloody fine tune your son's got." He then saw the look on Tony Blair's face, gave me back the phone, and went back to sit by the Prime Minister. I must admit I had a lot of respect for Neil

Kinnock after that incident.

The second time I interviewed Tony Blair, he was a little more relaxed. Although there were lots of protesters outside the building campaigning against the Gulf War, he was visibly calmer and more fun. The programme involved youngsters from various schools. I was one of two presenters who fronted the programme, and on this occasion, didn't ask him any questions of my own. Perhaps that's why he was more laid-back!

After the interview, he signed various pieces of memorabilia to give to the youngsters. Andy Miles was there with me, asking questions on behalf of Swansea Wave listeners. As we were sitting relaxing, pressman Alastair Campbell walked in.

"Good interview, chaps?" he asked. We answered in the affirmative, and I made a joke about his recent appearance on *Who Wants to be a Millionaire?* Campbell's next job was going off to South Africa as Press Officer for the British Lions' rugby tour.

"So, what's this Gavin Henson bloke like?" he asked. "I'll be spending quite a bit of time with him over the next few weeks." I replied, "I don't think you'll get on with him." When he asked me for clarification I told him, "The problem is, he used be Chairman of the Welsh Young Conservatives." Campbell looked visibly shaken. He wandered out of the room and I saw him walk up to Peter Hain. I could see the expression on Hain's face change, and I could make out that he was mouthing the word, "What?" As they both moved back into the room, Hain pointed towards me and said to Campbell, "Did he tell you that? He might be a Holy Roller, but don't believe a word he tells you. He's a wind-up merchant."

Just as Tony Blair couldn't predict my question, I often find that I don't know what a listener is going to say next. On one phone-in, I said to the new caller, "Where are you calling from?" – meaning which area of the city.

"What are you talking about? I'm in the house, mun! There's a boy, aye."

During the thirty years' celebrations for Swansea Sound, I was on air on a Bank Holiday Monday. It turned out to be thirty years to the day when Abba won the Eurovision Song Contest with 'Waterloo'. To mark the occasion I thought I would ask the listeners to vote for their favourite Abba song. The first caller said he was voting for 'Nikita'. I told him, "I think you'll find it should be 'Chiquitita'. 'Nikita' is an Elton John song." He said, "That's right. 'Nikita'. That's the one that gets my vote." And then he put the phone down.

The second caller said, "I'm voting for 'Angelo'."

"I think you'll find that was sung by the Brotherhood of Man. Don't you mean 'Fernando'?" I asked.

"Oh, yes, that's the one," he said and then he started to sing:

"Long ago, high on a mountain in Mexico,

Lived a young shepherd boy named Fernando."

The third caller said, "Hello." I replied, "Hello." There was a long pause.

"Hi," I said, trying to break the silence.

"Hi," she replied followed by another long period of quietness.

"So, what are you voting for?" I asked, trying to move the programme along.

"Labour," she replied, adding, "but I don't think it's any of your business!" And promptly put the phone down.

One day, a woman who won a competition on the radio said at the end of our interview, "Well there you are, Kevin, you've brought me some luck today. Let's hope you bring me some luck tonight with my Lotteries. Give me some numbers." Obligingly, I rattled off the first six numbers that came into my head.

Afterwards, Steve Barnes, our Programme Controller, said to me, "Are you going to back those numbers?" I was fairly dismissive of the idea, but then Steve countered by saying, "If those numbers come up, she'll be a millionaire and you'll have nothing." I must admit that I am not an avid player of the Lottery, or as she would have said, 'the Lotteries'. This is not because I have any moral or spiritual problems with the idea. I suppose my objections are more political and social. Being a Plasmarl boy from the east side of Swansea, I have always had difficulty with the idea of fat cats becoming wealthier and wealthier from money given by people who can barely afford it. In spite of such misgivings, I went to listen to the programme again and wrote down my numbers.

That afternoon, Rosie and I shopped in Tesco's at Llansamlet. I left her to pay, just in case the Switch card didn't go through(!), and I walked towards the car. As I passed the Lottery station I remembered the numbers. Filling in the form, I looked up, and there walking towards me was a deacon from the Pentecostal Church I attended as a boy. Deacons are like policemen, always there when you don't want them. And just to make matters worse, I didn't win. I suppose you've already guessed that, or else I wouldn't be writing this book!

My most embarrassing moment in broadcasting involves the wonderfully gifted comedian from Port Talbot, Rob Brydon. I do like people to like me when I'm interviewing them, and at the end of our chat, I have a spiel which runs along these lines:

"Thanks for all the pleasure you've given us over the years. Swansea has been made to feel all the better for your presence." I always finish by saying, "And may you have all the success you deserve in the future." I ran the interview with Rob between 8.30 and 9.00 a.m., which is peak time, with people listening on their way to work. Although I was enjoying it immensely, I knew I had to curtail the conversation as Traffic was waiting to come in.

"Well, that's all we've got time for now," I said. "Good luck in the Grand on Saturday." What my brain told me to say next was, "Rob, I wish you all the success you deserve in the future." Unfortunately, what my lips said was, "Rob, I wish you all the sex you deserve in the future." Slightly taken aback, he laughed, and in acute embarrassment, I said, "I'm sorry, Rob, I meant to say success." He replied, "I'll take the first one, if you don't mind.'

In addition to Rob Brydon, Radio has given me the

opportunity to interview many big names from the world of show business. Sometimes the person at the other end of the table turns out to be a childhood hero of mine. That was certainly the case when I interviewed Harry Secombe, who was appearing in *Pickwick* at the Swansea Grand Theatre. Harry was not well, and despite the fact that he had to drop out of several performances and let his understudy play his part, he managed to make it to the studios.

I first met him in the Eighties when I was asked to appear on a Christmas Special for the ITV *Highway* programme which Harry presented. The show was to be in front of a studio audience at Culverhouse Studios. I was asked to devise a magic trick for Christmas, so I came up with the idea of changing an umbrella into a Christmas tree. I rehearsed on the Saturday night but the following day, when I turned up for the recording, I was incredibly nervous. I felt even worse when I walked into the Green Room as it was full of big names that had filled my childhood: Clive Dunn, Roy Castle, Brian Johnston from *Test Match Special* and an opera singer who I was told was very famous, but I must admit I'd never heard of.

Suddenly the door burst open and in walked Harry Secombe. My nervous tension hit new heights with his arrival. Here I was in the presence of all these seasoned and famous entertainers, and now I was just a few feet away from the prize Goon who had shaped my childhood resolve to be a full-time entertainer. Harry marked his entrance with that high pitched "ha ha" greeting known to all lovers of the Goon Show programmes. As he saw me he gave me my own private "ha ha" and moving towards me said, "The Dynevor boy!" which, of course, was my old secondary school and the place where Harry had received his secondary education. I wasn't nervous after that.

One of my greatest joys in radio was to broadcast from the Universal Studios in Orlando, as part of a promotional trip organised by UCI Cinemas. I ended up interviewing 'Marilyn Monroe' and 'Beetlejuice', but I was left in no doubt whatsoever that I wasn't to ask them their real names. As far as I was concerned and they were concerned, they were the real characters. We were in Orlando for six days and I was booked to do three live shows. I would finish the programme at 9.00 a.m. and then I would have the rest of the day to enjoy the Sunshine State.

As I was interviewing 'Marilyn' one morning, Rosie, my wife, was travelling with my parents in the pouring rain with our two children to Carmarthen. The show was broadcast on Swansea Sound, so that Rosie heard 'Marilyn Monroe' saying in her sultry voice, "Hi, Kevin, it's lovely to see you again. You left the room very early this morning. That was such a lovely gift you left me on the pillow." Whilst I knew she was fabricating a story, that point was slightly lost on the sodden passengers in Carmarthen. When I phoned up later that day to speak to Rosie, I was met by a wall of silence.

While I was presenting these programmes, I ran a competition which gave the winner a family holiday in Orlando. Not all competitions on the radio end up as surreal as the Vote for your Favourite Abba Song. There is nothing more exciting than seeing and hearing the joy of a listener who has won a major prize.

In 2004 we ran a competition where listeners had to write in and say where they would like to holiday and why. It was won by a couple who had been married twenty-three years and never been on honeymoon. Lynne and Colin Hardwick were married in Creton near Northampton in 1981 and moved to live in Swansea in 1989. On the day of their wedding, Lynne was in a Northampton Hospital with severe back problems. She was allowed out for one-and-a-half hours, just enough time to get married, and then had to go back as a patient for several weeks. Unbeknown to Colin, Lynne had also applied for the prize. She chose Ireland and he chose Cyprus, which was to have been the honeymoon destination they had to cancel. In the end Colin won the day and they went to Cyprus.

I have been asked to do all sorts of things during radio broadcasts, and on one occasion, I ended up commentating on a live football match between Cheltenham and Swansea City. My son, Owain, had just finished his GCSE's and was working with the club. I drove him to the game, so that he could sit in the commentary box and write a report. The game was delayed for half an hour, due to a serious accident on the M5.

As we sat there, I received a phone call from Swansea Sound telling me that the commentator was stranded in traffic on the motorway. Madly, I offered to stand in. It was a total disaster. I couldn't keep up with the action and got quite a few names wrong. A couple of weeks later at the

Vetch, some fans came up to me and said, "We love you, Kev, and you're a great entertainer, but please promise us you will never commentate again."

I think I'll stick to the early day job!

CHAPTER FIVE

Football Fan-Tastic

OOTBALL. YOU EITHER HATE it or love it. I've been in the second category most of my life, although I like to think my obsession for all things football is not as bad as that of the late, great Bill Shankly's. When asked whether he thought football was a matter of life and death, the Liverpool manager replied in his craggy, Scottish accent, "No. It's much more important than that!"

I can console myself with the fact that I have many interests other than the round ball. Even so, there is something very special about being at a live match. Since 2006 I have acted in a football play about the Swans' golden era, called *Toshack or Me!*, and this speech by one of the characters, Dave, captures some of the feelings football gives me. Here, he describes his early visits to the Vetch:

"Thousands of people marching down to the ground. The streets full. The smell of the brewery, tobacco, hotdogs, and the floodlights dragging us in like moths. Then, after the game, all the old men reliving the moves, the misses, the goals. The air thick with suggestions for the players and the managers. It's always amazed me how the only people who don't know how to play are out there on the field.

"Then, on a Saturday, to climb the steps and see that beautiful, green pitch in front of you, like a rolled-out carpet. It's the best feeling in the world. Standing up high in the stand, it's like looking down on a human chess game – defences pushing forward, the attackers retreating. Moves and counter-moves and then in through the gap. Checkmate! Goal! Call it what you like. It's magic.

"OK, I suppose I've got a disease. And of all the illnesses I could have caught – Liverpool, Arsenal, Man United – I go down with the Swans!"

I caught the bug early on and I've been a football fan since I got my first football kit as a little boy. It was all blue, so I was told it was a Chelsea kit, although in those days teams didn't have advertising logos on their shirts. I wore it to bed that night.

I first started watching the Swans when I was seven years old. The first game I saw at the Vetch was a friendly between Swansea City and Newport County. I was well and truly bitten by the football bug. Every time I visited the Vetch I was shaking with excitement, and it's a feeling that all these years on is still with me. As a boy it was such a thrill to stand by the players' entrance and see players like my hero Vic Gomersall and the great George Best playing for Northern Ireland in the Home Internationals against Wales. I'd also watch great players like Ivor Allchurch who was in his last season for the Swans.

In those early days I used to stand on the North Bank, and I just fell in love with everything about those matches: the Swans, the football, the atmosphere and the great players

I saw. There were great characters who played for the team and captured my imagination; players like Tony Millington, who is now disabled and works for Wrexham Football Club as their Disability Officer. When Tony played, if the Swans were awarded a penalty, he would kneel down in the penalty area, turn his back on the action and pray for a goal. But he wouldn't be passive, he'd be working the fans and reacting to them.

Throughout the club's history, the players have always been close to the supporters. This was partly due to the compact nature of the Vetch. The pitch was so close to the terraces and the stands, it was inevitable that there would be a special atmosphere. I'm glad to say that this bond has continued at the Liberty Stadium.

Sadly, my own football career is not so illustrious. I played right back for Plasmarl Junior School, and that was followed by a couple of games for Hafod Comprehensive B Team. By the time I got to Dynevor School, I was one of the school theatricals. I quickly learned that the arty brigade didn't play football, and I also discovered that some of my fellow pupils were great players.

When I left school for London Bible College, I played for the team. Later, when I transferred to the Elim College (no fee involved), I played for them. Although a natural right back(!), I played my first game for Elim in goal. They stuck me between the posts because they reckoned I must have played rugby sometime in my life, so I should be able to hold the ball. Also, because I was bigger than anyone else, they hoped I'd fill the goal. It didn't work because we lost 13-0 to Millmead Baptist Church, Guildford. Not surprisingly, they moved me out of goal and I played up front, my only claim to fame being the fact that I scored five goals in one game.

When I moved back to Swansea from college, I appeared in a great number of charity football matches. On several occasions I played with Robbie James and Alan Curtis, arguably two of the Swans' greatest players. I started playing in the back but Robbie and Alan pushed me up front. Their reason for the tactical shift was that when I went up front from defence, I wasn't fit enough to run back when the opposition attacked. They felt it made more sense for me to go up front and stay there!

My most embarrassing football moment was playing in a charity football match at Aberavon's Talbot Athletic ground. It's not the best of surfaces to play on as it's really a rugby pitch. My son, Owain, who is a huge football fan, was watching from the stands with my father. I was playing for the Welsh Celebrity All Stars against The London All Stars (for whom I'd played previously). Emlyn Hughes, the ex-Liverpool and England player, was playing for the London team. I knew Emlyn, as just a few weeks before I had worked with him on a huge charity event in Warwickshire. The ball came to me and somehow I got past the defender and was suddenly one-on-one with the keeper. Emlyn Hughes came up behind me, shouting at the top of his voice, "Johns, you'll never score. You're fat and you're useless. You're rubbish." I started to laugh and I rounded the keeper and had the gaping goal at my mercy. All I had to do was score. I kicked the ball and the ground at the same time, missing an open goal. My son said it was the most embarrassing moment of his life.

My brief rugby career was even less illustrious. In one game I was clean through, heading for the touch line. The only thing I could hear was people shouting, "Go under the posts. Go under the posts." The aim was to make the conversion attempt easier. I looked to the side to see if my girl friend was watching from the sideline. Unfortunately, this distraction led to a serious misjudgement of the positioning of the posts, and I ran straight into them, dropping the ball. I was winded and the chance of an easy try went begging.

Being a life-long fan, watching the Swans has often been a mix of the best of times and the worst of times. Certainly one of the best seasons in their history must be 1980-1 when they were promoted to the top tier (the old First Division) for the first and only time. In the final game at Preston they needed to win to secure promotion. It was a difficult game, as the home team needed a victory to stay in the Second Division. In addition, if the Swans drew, Blackburn Rovers, who were playing at Bristol Rovers, would gain the final promotion place instead of the Swans. I was a student at London Bible College, and unfortunately, I missed the game, but not the celebrations.

There were four of us: Martin Wroe (now a journalist on one of the London broadsheets), his girlfriend, Meg, and my girlfriend at the time, Stephanie. We were walking on a golf course in Northwood, which is one of the better parts of the Home Counties. There was a public right of way through the course. As we walked on it we were listening to a radio commentary of the Swans' match at Preston. Martin was himself a Swansea boy, and when the final whistle was blown, we made such a noise we were asked by the golfers to leave the area.

I also missed the first home game in the top division when the Swans beat Leeds 5-1. I was working at a music festival in Knebworth. That year (1981), I had formed my own business as a children's entertainer and I was asked to run the Christmas party for the Swans' players and their families. All the stars from that promotion-winning side were present, including John Toshack, the manager, although he didn't watch my act. Despite being responsible for the entertainment, I felt like an excited school boy, especially when I came face to face with my hero, Vic Gomersall, and spoke to him for the first time in my life. Since that meeting, Vic, who is now Commercial Director at Llanelli, has become a close personal friend, with whom I have appeared in many charity football matches.

Of course, the experience of following a football club is rarely one of unparalleled success, and just five years after playing against the likes of Liverpool, Arsenal and Manchester United, we were back in the bottom division of the Football League (the old Fourth Division). In the Nineties we saw some success with a victory at Wembley in the Autoglass Trophy Final, followed by a near miss in the Play-Off Finals. The new millennium got off to a glorious start with the Swans winning the Third Division Championship.

It should have been one of the happiest days of my life.

The last Saturday of the football season and the long trek north to Rotherham had been rewarded with the Swans lifting the championship. It was not until I went into the Swansea Sound Studios the next day that I discovered Terry Coles, a life-long fan of the Swans, had been killed during trouble outside the stadium. My *Sunday Hotline* show was filled with callers paying heartfelt tributes to Terry. I was almost in tears throughout the programme. As often happens in such situations, the programme worked well and the management wanted to recommend it for an award. I refused out of respect for Terry.

The following Monday in front of a packed Vetch, Aston Villa, who were due to appear in the FA Cup Final the following Saturday, played the Swans in Keith Walker's Testimonial match. I had been told only that day that as the announcer at home matches and as the club chaplain, I would need to lead the crowd in a minute's silence. Standing in the centre circle, flanked by international stars David James and Gareth Southgate, it was one of the biggest challenges I had ever faced.

The following year, players and fans alike were to experience one of the greatest challenges faced by the club. The arrival of the Australian businessman Tony Petty as the new club owner was applauded by an unsuspecting crowd in a mid-week match at the Vetch in October 2001. Far from being the 'redeemer', he was to prove a threat to the very existence of Swansea Football Club.

For me, the difficulty with the Petty era was that I was involved with the Swans. I was doing all the entertainment on the pitch, but I was fundamentally opposed to the new regime at the club. So, when they formed the Swansea City Supporters' Trust, I found myself introducing all their meetings and became the Vice Chair. I was asked to lead the two marches through the city centre and speak at the supporters' rally in Castle Square.

When I first met Tony Petty I went eyeball-to-eyeball with him and said, "Don't you ruin my football club." He came for an interview on the *Sunday Hotline* which I was hosting for Swansea Sound. In some ways I felt sorry for him, because he took such a bashing from the fans. He was fundamentally very bad for Swansea City Football Club because he tried to get rid of players. All sorts of things happened during his time at the Vetch.

I got to one stage where I had had enough of the Petty problem. I didn't want to walk away from it, but I had reached a point where I felt overwhelmed by the crisis. I was involved with all kinds of meetings and organisations, without the club knowing. I was leading the marches, doing programmes on radio about the situation and supporting the fans as much as I could.

Then, someone phoned me and said, "Do you realise that you've been named as one of the members of Tony Petty's Supporters' Board?" This was a group he'd established in opposition to the Football Trust. I knew nothing about it. Someone was going around the city telling everyone that I was on this rebel board. I made a phone call to somebody and they could tell how angry I was. He rang David Morgan of the Supporters' Trust and said, "Get hold of Kevin Johns as quickly as you can. He's so angry I don't know what he's going to do."

That evening I went with my son to watch a match at Llanelli to get away from it all. Before the game we walked into the Jock Stein Bar. We sat down for a pork pie and sandwich and who should walk in with the Swans' manager, Colin Addison, but Tony Petty. There just seemed to be no way of getting away from him. He was a major problem.

I've never been able to figure why Petty got involved. When he arrived we were not terribly successful and we didn't own our own ground; it was owned by the Council. The new stadium was a long way from even being started. So what he would want from Swansea City Football Club, I'll never know. There were all sorts of stories that maybe he would bring in some Australian players and would sell them on because the market was better here than it was Down Under. Others felt that he may have thought the club was much bigger and more successful than it actually was. Whatever the reason, he came and bought it for a pound from Mike Lewis. He must have made some money out of it because he was a businessman. It was a dark time.

I remember going to a meeting at the Patti Pavilion and the spirit was absolutely amazing. It brought everyone together – fans and players. There were players at that meeting who were risking losing their jobs by being there because they were still employed by Swansea City Football Club.

There was one game against Rushden and Diamonds when Petty and his business partner were at the Vetch. For the entire match the fans barracked him. At the end of the game, I was near the Harry Griffiths bar. I'd been asked to go there because there were a few fans baying for blood. Fists had been thrown at Mike Lewis, who for many fans was as culpable for the mess at the Vetch as Tony Petty. I remember trying to put myself between some of the fans and Mike, because I felt whatever had happened, you shouldn't behave like that. But it just brought out the emotions in the supporters because we really did face extinction as a football club.

Mel Nurse, David Morgan and other members of the new Board became the saviours of football in Swansea. The Supporters' Club were magnificent then, but I suppose as the club has become stronger and safer, their role has changed. In the early days they were there to save the club. Eventually, they raised money to bring new players to the club, like Alan Tate and Leon Britton. But even with a new Board at the helm, there were still some dark days ahead.

The final day of the 2002-3 season dawned with Swansea City needing to beat Hull City. If the Swans had lost and Exeter had won, Swansea would have ceased being a professional Football League side. The weeks leading up to that final match were nerve-wracking. One life-long fan who lived in Moscow managed to borrow money from friends to fly over for the final match. He said he felt that he was coming to the bedside of a dying relative.

Another fan was not so lucky. He had watched the Swans ten times during the season and they had failed to win every time. His father, a retired policeman, threatened to circulate photographs of his son to all the stewards on the gate, so that he wouldn't gain access to the ground. The father was so convinced that he was a jinx on the club, he told his son to stay at home. The son obeyed and worked in the garden whilst his girlfriend listened to radio commentary indoors. On the two occasions he ventured inside, Hull City scored, and so he was told to leave the house and return to the garden! I suppose some would say it was good that he stayed away as Swansea won 4-2, and despite Exeter's victory, the Swans were safe. Before the game, I knew it was going to go down to the wire for the Swans. On the final Saturday I felt sick until the final whistle.

In 2008, I starred in a play about that season called *To Hull and Back*. Unlike many fans, I didn't resort to madcap plans to try and save the team, although I must admit I have a sneaking admiration for Vicar Joe, the character I played. It was uncanny how Peter Read, in writing Vicar Joe, seemed to replicate thoughts I had in the days leading up to the vital match against Hull. With a few days to go the end of the season, he decides he needs to get the Almighty on his side and prays this prayer:

"O Lord, when I read what you've been up to in your life story, you've done some pretty amazing things against the Canaanites and Amelakites and lots of other 'ites'. I'd like you to pull out all the stops next Saturday and destroy the Rochdale-ites. I wouldn't normally bother you over a matter as trifling as soccer. I usually leave it to the boys in white, but I think they need a bit of divine help this season.

"I know it seems a bit unfair on Rochdale. They haven't done anything wrong – unless you count the fact that a lot of their fans come from Eccles, where they make those cakes full of sugar and raisins and stuff. They're very bad for your teeth and I know you are keen on us looking after our bodies.

"I'd be grateful if you would pull a miracle out of the bag and help us win. It's really looking like it could go down to the wire, and I don't feel I've got the right sort of cutters. It's between Shrewsbury, Carlisle, Exeter and us. Any two, O Lord, from this sorry four will go out of the League. We've only got two games left. Rochdale, where, with your help, we'll give them a holy zapping, and then, the following week, Hull. I can't say much against them, except I wonder if you want a high profile team in the football league who are just one vowel away from hell. Hull... Hell! And I don't know if you've ever been there... of course, you have, you made the place. Well, they've made a terrible mess of what you gave them. It smells like a vat of Findus Fish Fingers gone off. Nothing like the Garden of Eden you intended. I know a couple of great poets were born there – Andrew Marvell and Philip Whatsisname... Larkin, but then again, it's given us John Prescott.

"And, as for Carlisle, well, I know it's a beautiful part of the world, but I wonder if you want to help a team with such a limited sense of imagination. They've got two nicknames: The Blues, because they play in blue, and the Cumbrians, because they come from Cumbria. And if I can bring in the question of justice, which I know you like, there were some very dodgy decisions in the game in March which helped them beat us. Otherwise we might be safe.

"Then there's Exeter. I'm not sure you should be supporting them. I'm not sure anyone should be supporting them. You see, their Chairman is Uri Geller. He's been on telly, bending spoons. I'm not really up on divine etiquette, but I'm sure you prefer your cutlery straight. Then there's the tricky question: how does he do it? Do you really want a team with an occultist at the helm still in the League? I should also mention that he's been enlisting the help of a few dodgy characters recently, like Michael Jackson and Mike Lewis, to name just a couple. Another problem with Exeter is their nickname – the Grecians. I know the Greeks gave us Philosophy and Mathematics and Grecian 2000, to cover my grey, but, if my memory serves me correctly, they didn't really help the spread of Christianity.

"And finally, O Lord, it looks like Yeovil are coming out of the Conference into the Football League. So, I think you should see it as a straight swap. One West Country team in and one West Country team out. I'm not really mentioning Shrewsbury because I think they could be a lost cause. Amen."

In fairness, since that unforgettable final day we haven't really had to take out the prayer mats. The Swans have gone from strength to strength and at the time of writing they have just been crowned Champions of League One and are now heading for the giddy heights of the Championship.

In many ways, the difficulties made us stronger as a club,

because it brought in the new Board – one full of committed Swansea City fans and intelligent and successful businessmen – and they've made the club the success it is today.

CHAPTER 6

The Man on the Mike

AT EVERY HOME MATCH at the Liberty Stadium I can be seen and heard welcoming the teams and whipping up the home fans into a frenzy of support. Again, I have made my fair share of mistakes in front of the big crowd. At the crucial last match of the 2002-3 football season when Swansea City played Hull City, ten thousand people crammed into the Vetch. The Swans needed to win the game to stay in the League. I had been asked to lead the crowd in a rendition of the Welsh National Anthem, *Hen Wlad Fy Nhadau*. Steve, who plays all the music at the games, told me to start as soon as I heard the CD playing. I was so pumped up that I convinced myself I'd heard the opening bars of our National Anthem. I could see Steve in his glass cubicle gesturing to tell me that he wasn't playing anything. It was too late by then. I had already pitched ten thousand people into the first few lines. We sang the whole anthem unaccompanied. Halfway through, I began to realise what I was doing and had a massive blood rush to my head. I thought I was going to die!

In a match against Macclesfield, I had to announce the substitutions, something which is normally left to Steve. He hadn't made it that evening because his wife had gone into labour just before kick-off. When I arrived at the ground I discovered I had no keys for the commentary box and there were none in the club office. It slowly dawned on me that one set would be in Steve's pocket at the hospital.

Jacky Rocky, the Club Secretary, looked at me and I looked at her. I could tell what she was thinking. There was no other option. I would very quickly have to learn a new skill, that of a cat burglar. Furthermore, I would have to hone the skills in front of thousands of bemused fans. Once I had broken in, which was frighteningly easy, and lumbered my way into the box, the difficult task was about to begin.

Walking onto the pitch and announcing the home side and building up the atmosphere was easy, but correctly announcing the names of the goal scorers and subs – that involved concentration! That's hard work.

Having already demonstrated at Cheltenham that I was not cut out for live football commentary, I was anxious to show that I was quite capable of reading out team changes. It would be very easy, wouldn't it? A piece of cake. I must admit that the sheet of paper from which I was working, splattered as it was with several crossings out and alterations, did suggest there may be a slight problem ahead. When I read out the final substitution for the visitors, their fans chanted, "Who?" And down on the touchline the fourth official was laughing. I had misread the list and sent on the referee by mistake!

Interestingly, I wouldn't have been in charge of the mike that day at the Vetch, or for any other match, if it were not for Pavarotti. The big man was making a guest appearance at the International Eisteddfod at Llangollen in 1995. Swansea Council decided to set up a giant screen in Singleton Park and show the concert live. The entertainment for the evening had been put in the hands of a company called Tactical Marketing. I had already done some work for them on a school project and was delighted to be involved in such a big event in my home town.

After the concert I did more work for them, compering the schools programme in places as diverse as Southampton, Newcastle, Glasgow, as well as many other British cities. Following the schools venture, Tactical Marketing was asked to organise events for Coca Cola. That partnership led to me fronting a whole range of events, including a one-on-one basketball competition for Sprite in Battersea Park.

For the Coca Cola Cup Final hospitality at the Wembley Bowl, they built a mock structure of Wembley Stadium's Twin Towers. This was the front piece for a penalty shoot-out competition using Subbuteo footballers. It was hilarious watching people trying to show off their immense footballing skills with tiny models. The miniscule ball would end up a million miles away from the goal and there were several incidents of severely broken footballers. I would dress up as a football referee, and arguably one of my most bizarre moments was weeing into a urinal dressed as a football ref standing next to David Baddiel. Having an official in such close proximity, it was only a matter of time before he was going to have a go at me.

The Subbuteo penalty shoot-outs played a major part of

the pre-match entertainment in the hospitality suite before the Coca Cola Cup Finals at Wembley. Everyone had a go and it was great to watch children pit their wits and skills against the celebrities.

The final between Leicester City and Middlesbrough at Wembley in 1997, which Leicester won after extra time, was the first major final for which I did the entertainment, followed by the 1998 final again involving Middlesbrough, although this time Chelsea won 2-0 after extra time.

In 1999, sponsorship was taken over by Worthington's and I worked for them at the 1999 final between Spurs and Leicester City, which the London team won 1-0. That year I was asked to be part of the half-time entertainment, and although I had led the Swans' fans' singing during the play-off final against Northampton at Wembley in 1997, it was still an awesome experience to work the Wembley turf in front of a full house.

The first Worthington Cup Final (1999) saw Leicester City beat the underdogs, Tranmere Rovers 2-1. Having lived in Birkenhead, the home of Tranmere Rovers, I had a soft spot for the Merseyside team, and I was lucky to be given a ticket to watch the whole match.

In the following year, there was an important change as all the major finals and sporting events switched to the Millennium Stadium in Cardiff. Once Worthington took over, the events became more fan-centred. I was asked to run a fans' football tournament, called the Worthington Fives. Every club in the Football League was asked to form a fans' football team. We had a northern event in Manchester and the southern teams played each other at an event in Slough. After those events, the teams who were still standing would come to an event at the five-a-side stadium in Nottingham. It was a fantastic tournament, and I met wonderful fans from all over England and Wales. Talking to lifelong supporters of other teams made me realise there should be no room for nastiness and aggression amongst supporters of different teams. Fans are fans wherever they come from. I worked with and had fun with fans of every team in the League and the Premiership.

During these tournaments, I was lucky enough to meet many great names from the world of football. One of the nicest characters I've met is Graham Taylor. For a Welshman to say that is quite incredible, because he was, of course, manager of England. Graham Taylor is a man of great dignity and also possesses a wonderful football mind.

As well as meeting greats from the world of sport, the tournaments were memorable for the way they could turn the form book of clubs upside down and inside out. On one occasion, Kidderminster Harriers, who hadn't long been promoted to the League from non-league football, were drawn to play against the might of Manchester United. When we came to play the game all the Man United players turned up in matching kits and MUTV, the club's own television station, came to record the contest. The top team in the league was playing one of the bottom teams. The final score was Manchester United 1 Kidderminster Harriers 15.

Another time, we had just completed the first round matches at the Power League Centre in Manchester. It is a great facility but it's in one of the less salubrious areas of the city. We were waiting for a phone call to tell us the details of the second round draw. I had been there since eight o'clock in the morning and was aware that several other groups were using the facility. It was now four o'clock and we were standing in the car park waiting for the news. Suddenly there was the sound of screeching car tyres and a police car siren. We all ran up the nearby grass bank to have a better view of what was happening. As we reached the summit we heard gun shots. We all dropped like stones and hit the deck, or more accurately, the mud. As we lay face down, all of us terrified for our lives, I heard someone shout, "Cut!" One of the groups using the centre was a film crew. We walked back down the bank covered in mud, ready for the announcement of Round Two.

I ran these tournaments for four years and it meant that for the first Worthington Fives' final I got to do some pre-match entertainment on the pitch at Wembley before the Spurs and Leicester game. Although it wasn't a great match, for me, it was a thrill to be taking part in a final at one of the finest stadiums in the world. Before the match there was a piece in the *Evening Post* delighting in the fact that Swansea would be represented at a major Cup Final in Wembley by a Swansea presence – me!

After leading the singing at Wembley for the Swans Play-Off Final in 1999, I received a call from Swansea City asking me why I wasn't doing similar pre-match entertainment at the Vetch. This was to be a new departure for the Swans, as it was for me. In the past, any input before a match had tended to come from an announcer in the commentary box. We were now going into uncharted territory with someone entertaining the crowd from the pitch. It meant that I was free to develop my brief in whichever way I wanted.

In the ten years I have brandished the mike at the games, we have seen the emergence of penalty shoot-outs and games between the Swansea Schools of Excellence. Previously, some people had come onto the pitch before a match to do a prize draw, but no one had ever combined announcing with entertainment. The first game in which I was in charge of the mike was a Swans match against Exeter City at the start of the 1997-8 season. The Devon side boasted a famous director in Uri Geller. As he was at the game, I introduced him on the pitch and took him over to the North Bank where we challenged him to bend a spoon.

It has been great working with youngsters on the pitch before the football action starts. On one occasion, a youngster who was something of a gymnast, took a penalty against the Swans' mascot, Cyril the Swan. When he scored, he celebrated in the way which has now been made famous by professional players. He did several athletic looking flops, rolls and cartwheels. The fans loved it and gave him great applause. When he'd finished I said, "Well done, you cheeky show off. Come back here." I then made him run to the other end of the pitch to take a penalty. That's become something of a trademark of our pitch entertainment ever since.

The prank seriously backfired when on one occasion a member of staff discovered it was my birthday. He came on to the pitch, took the mike and then made me run the entire length of the pitch to take a penalty. I had lost some weight and I remember thinking near the penalty spot, I must pull my trousers up, or else they're going to end up around my ankles! When I eventually reached the ball, I whacked it with all the energy I could muster and it was a marvellous feeling to see the ball whiz past Cyril the Swan and thud into the back of the net. I jumped onto the wall of the East Stand to milk the celebration and our Swansea Sound commentator, Anthony O'Connell, did a commentary on air. I still treasure the copy of the recording of that moment which he gave me.

I never script or think too much about what I am going to say once I have the mike. It is all very much 'off-the-cuff' and that gives me the freedom to have fun. Before one match, the players were on the pitch warming up. Leon Britton, who is very small, was having a kick around with his team mates. He happened to be standing very near to where the children were lining up to take penalties against Cyril.

"There we are," I said. "All done... Wait a minute there's a little boy here who hasn't had a shot yet. Oh, sorry, Britts, it's you," I added, looking at Leon! Mercifully, he has a great sense of humour, and I believe that in the future he will join the Swans' Hall of Fame amongst other wonderful players, such as Alan Curtis and Ivor Allchurch.

I believe it is important that the entertainment is done by a Swans' fan. I was once touted to do the pre-match entertainment at a Premiership Club. I wasn't told who the club was, but they had watched me in action and liked what I did. Most clubs in the top flight pay for their person on the mike. I don't get paid at the Liberty Stadium. I do it because of my love for the Swans. It also means that once I have finished, I can go and sit down and watch the match with my father and son.

As the man with the mike, I have stood on the wall of the North Bank, waving a scarf above my head, leading the fans as they sang 'Delilah'. I wouldn't have done that if I was just a professional performer from another town who had no great feelings for the Swans. That was why I decided against pursuing the interest from the Premiership.

For the last game at the Vetch against Shrewsbury, I asked the wonderful singer Cath Davies to lead a singsong before the match. I had worked with her in pantomime and in the musical *Amazing Grace*. When she arrived at the ground, she was wearing a frighteningly revealing top. As soon as I saw her and it, I predicted that when the fans spotted Cath they would break into chants and songs inviting her to get something out for the boys. Her father said, "I've told her, as well," but she was adamant that everything would be fine. As she walked out onto the pitch and the crowd responded, I thought to myself, "Well, I did tell her." Someone gave her a black and white scarf and she eventually used it to cover her boobs for 'My Way'.

People often say to me, "I would love to do what you do on the pitch." My response to that is always, "Why do you want to do it? Is it because you love Swansea City and want to do something for them, or is it because you want to be part of the buzz?"

When I finish the mike work at the match, I go and sit with the same people every game: Dad, Owain, my friends, Chris, Matthew, John and Steph. I don't swan around, flashing my pass trying to suck up to the important people. I go back to my seat and when I leave the ground at the end of the game, I go through the same exits as every other fan. As far as I'm concerned, I'm just an ordinary fan helping the Swans in whatever way I can. I'm not there to be close to people running a football club. I am there because I want to be there. I was there when we nearly went out of the Football League and I'll be there when we're pressing for the Premiership in the future. If the day comes when the powers that be feel they no longer need my pre-match entertainment, then I will buy my season ticket and carry on watching them with my friends, my dad and son.

We had great fun when every club used to bring their mascot to the Vetch. We would organise a penalty shoot-out between Cyril and the visiting mascot. It no longer happens because Cyril always used to beat them. There are some fascinating and memorable mascots dotted around the League clubs, but I will never forget the day the Millwall Lion came to take his penalties against Cyril. Cyril, who has since matured a little, was in his cheeky, adolescent phase. As the Lion took the penalty, his head fell off. Cyril picked it up and punted it towards the fans on the North Bank. Someone phoned Five Live claiming that Cyril had knocked his head off, which is a fabrication. Even Cyril would not have done that! Though I have to admit that looking after him was a full-time job.

During one season when Swansea was playing Hull City at the Vetch, the game was delayed by about thirty minutes. There had been a torrential downpour and water had to be swept off the pitch before the game could start. One of the Hull fans threw something into the North Bank. It was not a good thing to do, especially as the fans had been in the ground a long time without seeing any action. People were becoming frustrated and tempers were well and truly frayed. Some of the Swans' fans spilled onto the pitch and headed towards the Hull fans. The only people on the pitch were Cyril the Swan and me. We were the buffer between the two sets of fans. We managed to talk to them, and mercifully, they listened and went back into the stand.

After the match I was touched by the fact that the Chairman of the club came and thanked us for what we had done. I will also never forget the thrill of hearing the North Bank singing, "There's only one Kevin Johns." The lyrics might not be the most earth-shattering or the finest that have ever been written, but I must admit that on that day they were music to my ears.

When the Ospreys rugby team moved to the Liberty Stadium, they asked me to do the pre-match entertainment on a regular basis. The only reason I refused is that I am not a rugby fan. I also didn't think it fair on my family that I would be missing for another set of Saturdays, plus certain mid-week matches. Whilst I like most sports, I don't have the same passion for the Ospreys as I do for the Swans, and I think that would have shown in my performances. If all the

Welsh rugby clubs are doing well then I'm delighted, but I have to admit that, on the day Wales won the Grand Slam and the Swans lost to Northampton in 2008, if you had said I could only choose one result, then I would have chosen three points at Northampton. Of course, I wanted both to win, but my real passion is football.

Llanelli Rugby Club also asked me to take control of their mike. Again I refused, owing to my commitments and the amount of theatre work I was doing at the time. When they became the regional side, the Scarlets, they asked me again, and I agreed to do it for one or two matches, so that they could see the kind of things I did and said in the warm up. Having seen me in action they would then appoint a Scarlets' fan, which is what they've done.

Before one of the matches, the Scarlets' choir came onto the pitch to sing. When they finished I congratulated them by saying, "Well done to the Scarlets' choir for showing the wide variety of sizes that you can get your club shirt in. Small, Medium, Large, Extra Large and Duvet size." There is nothing quite as gratifying as hearing a full stadium roaring with laughter at something you have just said.

Before another match at Stradey Park, I was walking from the pitch into the Enclosure. The players were warming up and someone shouted, "Incoming!" I ducked and a rugby ball flew over my head. Once in the Enclosure, I started talking to a fan who had two pints of beer on the wall of the stand in front of him. We chatted about pantomime, Swansea Sound, Swansea City and lots of other issues. Again someone shouted, "Incoming!" I turned around and realised that the ball was heading straight for us. The man could see that the ball was coming his way. He looked at his beer on the wall and he looked at his eleven-year-old daughter sitting next to him. He looked at the ball. He looked at his daughter. Then he threw himself forward to make a human shield... over his beer. The ball missed the beer as he had hoped, but hit his daughter on the head. She started to cry. I looked at him, slightly amazed. Returning my stare he said, "Aye, but the trouble is, see, I'd have to queue up for some more beer. Come here, love."

I enjoy building up a relationship with fans, even when they are as unpredictable and unusual as he was. At the Liberty Stadium, I park my car and take ages to get into the ground because I end up talking to almost everyone. I think this is why my work on the mike and all the work I have done for Swansea City has been successful. It's because I'm not an outsider doing a job of work. I feel I am part of the club and part of the Swans. I am proud of that club and excited by the way the Swans' fans have taken me to their hearts.

CHAPTER 7

Small Change for Big Change

GROWING UP AS A child in a caring family, I learnt the ethics and importance of charity work. My mother was a social worker, and as a youngster, I used to help her organise events for the disabled and the elderly. My father was also a volunteer, driving ambulances for the Multiple Sclerosis Society.

The first voluntary work I did was when I was in the Sixth Form at Dynevor School. We came up with the idea of writing a booklet on the best facilities in Swansea for disabled people. One of our group, Janet Elias, decided that she would sit in a wheelchair as we went around the city. The pushers would discover how easy or difficult it was to gain access to city centre premises. We pushed her into one café on the High Street and a waitress said, "You can't bring those in here." So I tapped Janet on the shoulder and she jumped out of the chair and walked out of the premises. As we followed her with the wheelchair, the owner chased us out of the property shouting, "What's going on?" When we explained our project to her, she invited us back in. So her café moved very quickly from the negative to the positive column.

After that first taste of volunteering, I joined the MS Society as a volunteer. Through that organisation I met some of the most incredible people who helped to shape the rest of my life.

My hope is that this chapter will draw attention to the thousands of wonderful people who do marvellous work for charities in this country. The voluntary sector is full of individuals who do a full day's work and then do another day's work for their charity free of charge. They save the economy millions of pounds using their skills, some of which are passed on to others. In addition to these stalwarts, there are children as young as seven who act as carers for disabled parents. Compared with these people, my work is nothing.

Some performers will put on their publicity that they have raised millions for charity. I have no idea how much I have collected as I never keep a record. In an auction I can often bring in £20,000 to the charity within half an hour. That doesn't go on my CV, because as far as I am concerned, I haven't raised it; it's the generous donors and the hardworking organisers who have raised the money. There are thousands of people who have done far more work for charity than I have. This chapter is about them and the brave sufferers who benefit from the work of the charity. It is not about me.

I have to admit that I enjoy the charity work I do. On one occasion I was involved in an event for McDonald's. It was a golfing day and I had to dress in 1920s golf attire. Part of my brief was to interview all the competitors who were also wearing the same style of clothes. As I talked to them we were being filmed for a video, a copy of which was to be given to everyone who had taken part.

My day had started with a 5 a.m. departure from my home followed by a long drive to Warwickshire. The day would not finish until one o'clock the following morning, so it was going to be very long. Everything went well with the 'Heads and Tails' game and the raffle bringing in lots of money. The auction was particular fun. One of the guests – who was drunk – paid £4,000 for a garden makeover. The following year at the same event he came up to me and said, "You caught me last year."

"Did I?" I asked innocently.

"You made me pay £4,000 for a garden makeover."

"Did I?" I repeated, this time my innocent voice sounding a little thinner.

"Yes, you did. My wife went absolutely mad. You won't catch me this year," he said.

"Well, don't drink then," I advised. He went away full of resolve but I caught him yet again. The auction, which lasted for thirty minutes, raised £18,000 – not all from him!

I am always amazed by people's generosity at these events. Whilst many feel that the donors must be able to afford what they have given, I have been at events where people have given the equivalent of the Widow's Mite to help a cause in which they believe passionately. I work on the assumption that no one needs to give anything to anyone, so I am always impressed when people give to charity whether they are wealthy or not. There are a lot of people in Britain who are wealthy because they don't give anything away.

At the end of the penultimate performance of my first pantomime at the Swansea Grand Theatre, I was stunned to see some people walking on the stage. They turned out to be Help The Aged staff who came up to present me with an award for the Welsh Celebrity Fundraiser of the Year. I won the award in two consecutive years, 1997 and 1998, and it meant a lot to me that I had been able to help them raise so much money for such a vital cause.

Raising money for charity has actually helped my health. When I was asked to raise funds for the British Heart Foundation, I realised that at 5 foot 6 inches and eighteen and a half stone, I was in danger of becoming a beneficiary of the organisation, rather than a helper. I looked at a photograph of myself and thought, "You are a fat bugger." I decided that I didn't want to be fat for the rest of my life. The characters I was playing in pantomime and on stage were obviously cover for the fact that I was overweight. Despite my condition, I was still able to move fairly well on stage. Throughout my career I have come across several actors and performers who are good movers, despite the fact that they are podgy!

Rob Clarke, who has a personal training business in Gorseinon, contacted me to ask whether he could help me in any way. He had seen an article in the local paper in which I stated my desire to lose weight. Working with Rob and keeping food diaries helped me to come down from eighteen and a half stone to fourteen stone. He gave me terrific support, and on the first 10k charity run I did, Rob insisted that he accompany me. He was much fitter and faster than me, but he ran alongside and never left me. I also did the Gower Bike Ride with him. It has been a fantastic achievement to run three 10k races and to successfully compete in and complete two Gower Bike Rides. Whilst all these events have made me feel good about my new figure, they have also enabled me to raise money for charity.

It was definitely a case that if I could lose weight anyone could, because I have always had a huge problem resisting food. I think everyone has the potential to become an addict and for me the addiction was food. I'm just grateful I don't drink and that I have never been enticed to take drugs, because I know that I have an obsessive nature.

I was certainly obsessed with eating. I would do a job during the day and be hungry at the end of it. On my way home I would call in the petrol station and buy something to eat. An hour later I'd be sitting down to my meal at home. My lifestyle certainly didn't help. In the morning I would have an early breakfast before doing the Morning Show at six o'clock. When I finished at ten o'clock I would be starving hungry. Following my two breakfasts I would then be ready for lunch.

Being on the after-dinner circuit also fuelled my addiction. After speaking at an event in a far-away place such as Manchester, whilst driving home to Swansea, I would inevitably stop at a garage and buy something to eat for the long journey home.

Since losing weight, I have done all kinds of scary things

such as abseiling off the top of the *Evening Post* building in Swansea. I have also flown a glider. My desire to run the annual 10k race and to participate in the Gower Bike Ride were what forced me to shed the pounds. The Gower Bike Ride covers a distance of twenty-nine miles and I had this wonderful idea that I would cycle from the Swansea Sound studios in Gorseinon to the start of the race. Once I had finished my first Sunday morning show, I cycled to the starting point and had an hour's rest before presenting *The Sunday Hotline*. I did the twenty-nine mile circuit and then it dawned on me that I would have to cycle another seven miles home! So that day, instead of doing twenty-nine miles for charity, I ended up doing a total of forty-three. I wish I could say how good it was to be keeping fit out in the open air and how self-righteous I felt keeping my body in trim. The truth of the matter is that those extra fourteen miles nearly killed me!

There is little to beat the joy of handing over a large cheque to organisers, knowing that the money will be used to aid those who are suffering. Despite that thrill there are days when a little sensible voice inside your head whispers, "Why are you doing this?" I must admit, the day I went up in a glider for charity, I was terrified. It didn't help that when I got inside the machine, I was already feeling sick. As I looked down at the far-away earth, I began to think about how fragile the glider actually was. I also became aware of how fast we were heading for the ground, and I convinced myself that we were going to crash.

Over the years, I have abseiled on many occasions. I

do it now without thinking and it gives me a wonderful sensation. On my first attempt, however, I didn't feel quite so comfortable. I had agreed to abseil off the top of the *Evening Post* building in Adelaide Street in Swansea to raise money for Help the Aged. My son, Owain, came to support me. As he stood watching the other volunteers coming off the top of the building, he looked at me and said, "Oh, goodness, Dad, you're going to die!"

Recently, I abseiled off the top of Princess House in Swansea, one of the tallest buildings in the city. As I was clambering up, someone asked me if I was feeling nervous. I foolishly replied, "No," pointing out that I was an old hand at this, having abseiled the *Evening Post*. When I arrived at the top I became aware of the incredibly strong wind. I then looked down and saw the dot of the *Evening Post* office down below. It struck me how small it was in comparison with the structure I was about to throw myself off. The person before me had all the gear, looked ultra professional and was much younger. He got over the side, froze, then hauled himself back up onto the rooftop. He just couldn't do it. Such lack of confidence and the presence of sheer fear in the face of someone else was the worst kind of preparation for my death-defying performance. My nerves were calmed by the fact that the non-jumper was followed by a seventy-five year old lady. Hurtling through the atmosphere, I reminded myself that this was a wonderful sport!

A few years ago, I decided that instead of working for several charities, I would concentrate on just one. This was about the time my financial adviser told me that if I didn't cut down on my charity work and start earning serious money, I would soon be a charity case myself. Therefore, it made sense to channel all my energies into the one organisation.

I had been raising money for the Christian Lewis Trust by doing the entertainment at their children's parties. The Trust is a wonderful society which helps children who have cancer and supports their parents. It organises holidays and also gives financial aid to those families who are in need. In addition, it offers play therapy for children suffering from leukaemia and their brothers and sisters.

A friend of mine who was on the board of executives asked me to become a trustee. What I didn't know when I made this decision was that a few years later there would be major problems within the Christian Lewis Trust. The police were called in to investigate the finances of the organisation.

While I was performing in *Aladdin* at the Swansea Grand Theatre in 2000, I received a phone call to tell me the Trust was in considerable debt and that as a trustee, I could end up paying my share. This came as a terrible shock as I, along with most of the other trustees, believed the organisation's finances were in credit. The caller urged me to attend the next trustees' meeting and reminded me to bring my cheque book! In the end I had to borrow £7,500 as a contribution towards the debt. Others paid considerably more but that was the maximum sum I was allowed to borrow at the time. It was a very worrying period and I was one of the people who asked for the police to investigate. There was no prosecution as it was felt it would not be in the public's interest.

It was such a worrying time that I developed psoriasis and high blood pressure and still suffer today. After that disaster I am glad to say that through the hard work of many of the members, the group is once again back on its feet and functioning as a charity. It was a very stressful time for my family and me. I am not a trustee any more as everything is now in place to make the Trust function. They continue with a wonderful and dedicated staff to carry out excellent work with children who have cancer and their families.

Since the problems with the Christian Lewis Trust, I no longer concentrate on just one charity. This has meant that once again, I suffer from the problem of finding it difficult to say no. I feel a great sense of responsibility because Swansea as a city has been extremely good to me. It's a great place in which to live, and audiences seem to like what I do and are appreciative of all my performances. In addition, the city paid for me to go away and study and it has also educated my two children extremely well.

Almost all the work I do for charities is free, although sometimes I get travelling expenses or a small fee. I understand that all the organisations I help are often trying to operate on a budget which is much smaller than the one they need to deliver their services.

I suppose I have become famous at charity events for my loud, booming voice. I am the one who calls everyone to order and gets the show on the road. In summer 2007, however, I did an event in Cardiff, where – owing to the poor public address system – I ended up hoarse. For several weeks my voice remained in a poor condition. It failed to recover and subsequently I had to cancel a few important engagements. Tests on my voice proved that I had a benign stricture which caused acidic burning of my voice area. It took a long time to heal and recover.

When the doctor said, "We think it's benign but we want to carry out tests just to make sure," I was very worried, as such a statement inevitably brings with it a whole stack of other worries. I genuinely thought that my career was over. It was not until March 2008 that I had the medical all clear, and it was a further month before I was able to say that my voice was back to normal.

Making a living as an entertainer and helping charities as much as I can is a very tricky balancing act. I suppose word has got around that Kev will always say yes. It's particularly galling when you turn up for nothing and no one has the decency to thank you. That has happened a few times and I have to say that on some occasions it is the major charities which have been guilty. After such events, I go home and say to Rosie, "I won't be doing that one next year." On the whole, however, people who organise such events are very friendly and appreciative of your support.

Most of the time, I am glad to help as I know there is not a vast amount of money around in Swansea. This becomes apparent at events when I notice that it is the same small group of people who are buying over and over again.

I once did a fundraiser for the Ivor Allchurch statue which now stands outside the Liberty Stadium. The event was held at the Rugby Club in St Helens. As I looked around the room I realised that the majority of people present were very young. They couldn't possibly have remembered him playing, as he ended his career in the late Sixties. I was stunned by the generosity of these young people who, in addition to not knowing the great man, probably had very little money to throw around. I continue to be amazed by the generosity of people locally.

Charity work has given me the opportunity to attempt many new challenges. Looking back on my life, I suppose there are lots of contenders in the Greatest Achievement category and most of them involve dance. In my mind I have always been a dancer and a huge regret is that I never studied dance. I love everything about it – the dancing and the dancers. I would have loved to have made it as a dancer, which I know will make people laugh, but I don't care.

Theatr Penyrheol, Gorseinon, where I have often worked and which is my local theatre, contacted me to say that they were organising a *Strictly Come Dancing* event for the Gorseinon Arts Festival, and they wondered whether I would be interested in taking part. Various couples from the area would be competing. When they asked who I would like to partner, I chose my daughter, Bethan. Unlike me, she had some dance skills in that she could do Tap and Jazz but had no experience in Ballroom Dancing. Together we went to Dance Kingdom in Llanelli and under their expert tuition, we learnt the Waltz, Jive and the Rumba within six weeks.

We all came together for a wonderful evening in Gorseinon where there were over four hundred people watching. We had to dance our three dances in front of judges. At the end of the adjudication the top three couples were selected for the final, when they would perform their favourite dance. I found the Waltz very difficult, so sadly, after that particular dance, we weren't in the top three. Then came our Rumba which suddenly put us in with a shout of qualifying for the final.

Our last dance, the Jive, was something special. I knew that of the three it was the only one into which I could put something of myself. It was a great success and we almost gained maximum marks. With our accumulated marks it was good enough to put us in the final. We repeated our Jive, and despite stiff opposition from a couple of waltzers and two other jivers, we won the competition. It was great to win and at the same time help the charity.

To see the look of joy on my daughter's face and the faces of family and friends was something I will always remember. We were given a huge trophy which I have never seen since that night because it disappeared into my daughter's bedroom! I felt so exhilarated, as I had achieved something which for a long time in my life I had felt was unachievable.

I am not one to look back on my life and wish it had been different, as I am very happy, but I suppose I would have liked more opportunity to dance professionally. As a child in my front room in Plasmarl I used to listen to and watch Fred Astaire and Ginger Rogers. I was captivated by their movement.

As well as supporting charities which exist to alleviate suffering, I will also rally round anything which supports

Swansea. That's why I was prepared to front a charity concert at the Brangwyn Hall in support of The National Assembly being based in Swansea. The then Secretary of State for Wales, Ron Davies, who had worked hard to champion devolution, invited the cities of Wales to put forward a case for housing the Assembly. I believed that Swansea had the best argument. We had a great evening. Dafydd Ellis Thomas spoke and we had music from the excellent Swansea band, Boys From The Hill, and Mal Pope.

While this campaign was raging, I fronted a dinner in Cardiff and introduced myself as coming from the future home of the Welsh Assembly. People shouted out, "You can have it!" There was little appetite in the capital for the Assembly.

I campaigned for it because it was a multi-party issue; as a public entertainer, I am always at pains not to show my political allegiance. This is an issue which I have always felt passionately about. I gave my first speech in favour of devolution at the age of thirteen in front of the Dynevor School Debating Society.

I have a great passion for Swansea which is matched by my love for Wales as a whole. Having lived in the north and south of Wales, I believe that now we have a devolved government there is a need for someone to unite the two halves of this great country of ours. Perhaps it would help if in the future the First Minister came from north Wales.

Whilst there was some disappointment that the Senedd didn't come to Swansea, I believe that all the good things that are happening to Swansea now are a direct result of the vote in favour of devolution. We have a bustling city which is a great place to live and I believe it will be one of the great cities of Europe in the future.

I am happy that in a very small way, I was able to help raise money to give this city a greater profile and to support individuals from Swansea in need of financial assistance.

CHAPTER 8

Treading the Boards at Last!

A S A YOUNGSTER, THE only thing I ever wanted to be was an actor and a performer. At school we didn't have a drama department, but we had a fantastic English department, plus a very fine music section that got all the children involved in school shows. We staged plays such as *The Government Inspector* and like many schools in the Seventies, put on a major production of *Joseph and the Amazing Technicolour Dreamcoat*. We also staged *Godspell*. All of these were quite challenging roles for young actors.

We had a first class English teacher called David Taylor who still comes to see me perform today. He and Johnny Morris, the music teacher, were probably the two greatest influences on my life outside my family. Their support has definitely guided and helped me along the way.

The plan which drove me during those early years was to leave school and seek employment as an actor. When I was seventeen, I was asked to go and perform in *Joseph* for the summer season at Aberystwyth. My parents, however, were reluctant to let me go, and as I was under eighteen, they had every right to stop me. As I look back on that time, I think that may have been a missed opportunity, although I have no regrets.

When I left school, I enrolled as a student at the London Bible College, which as I have already said, threw all my plans upside down. Despite the change in direction, the first thing I did when I arrived at the college was to sign up for The Christian Work Certificate, alongside the Cambridge University Diploma, rather than the Christian Ministry Diploma. This meant that I was able to join the College Drama Team which provided me with wonderful training for any performances I would do in the future. For a start, very few professional actors would ever have an opportunity to work in the places in which I acted.

We gave the group the name The Alias Drama Company and performed at venues such as the Oxford Kilburn Club. The group was run by a group of ex-Oxford students who felt that they wanted to do some kind of outreach work in Kilburn, which is a very rough part of London. We performed after the five-a-side tournament which the students organised. My first theatre audiences, therefore, were not the sophisticated chattering classes of the West End, but tough children from a very deprived area of London.

We also did Street Theatre in Watford. If you can work an audience on Watford's streets on a Saturday morning, then it equips you for all the acting challenges of the future. We also performed in some of the London markets, such as Petticoat Lane and those in the West End. Often, I would look up at the bright lights of 'Theatre Land' and think how nice it would be to work those theatres rather than perform on the streets to people who were on their way to see bigger and brighter productions than we could ever offer. Despite the disparity between the two worlds, I know that I received many of the elements of training that professional actors receive in Drama College.

Nowadays, when I appear in professional theatre and am relaxing with the actors, it is inevitable that one of the topics of conversation will be where we all trained. As soon as the discussion starts I stand up and offer to make everyone a nice cup of tea. Nearing the door complete with orders, I hear, "I went to the Royal College of Music and Drama," or "Rose Bruford," or "I studied at RADA." Before they can say, "Where did you train, Kev?" I'm clarifying whether it's two sugars or none and with or without milk. Such talk can often make me feel slightly insecure as an actor.

It has taken me quite a while to gain confidence in my own acting ability. I have always felt comfortable about playing a comedic part or the Dame in pantomime, but when I am standing on stage alongside highly-trained and experienced actors, I feel that I have to prove that I have a right to be there. There are some who look down their noses at the thespian from Plasmarl, but on the whole, the encouragement and support I have received from fellow actors has been absolutely great. They are always very willing to help out and point me in the right direction whenever I am struggling. In most of the plays I have been in, I have found that there is a team spirit and a company spirit which I love.

Other than pantomime, the first theatre play in which I acted was at the Swansea Grand Theatre. It was only a small part for the repertory company, Ian Dickens Productions. They asked me to appear in the very funny farce by Ray Cooney, called *Run For Your Wife*. The contract was for one week only as another actor played my part in other venues. It was a star-studded cast with actors such as Sophie Lawrence, David Callister and Eric Potts, who is fairly well-known as a *Coronation Street* actor. Jeffrey Holland, who was in *Hi De Hi!* was also in the show.

I was quite nervous going into that production because my name was billed above some I consider to be incredible actors. I had very little rehearsal time as they were on tour and had asked me to stand in just for the Swansea week. I was to play the part of a tabloid journalist. The play is one of those door-slamming comedies where people are constantly coming in and out and trying to hide things from other characters.

I think we do traditional farce extremely well in Britain, and no one can do it better than Ray Cooney, who in my opinion is the absolute master of writing this type of material. In America during the Sixties, they tried to emulate British farce with shows such as *How to Succeed in Business* and other musical farces, but what they produced was never as good as what we can churn out in Britain.

For me, David Callister, who outside of the business is not terribly well known, is without doubt the finest actor of farce I've ever encountered. When I was involved with *Peter Pan* at the Grand, he stood in for John Challis, who had to take a day off to film a Christmas Special for *Only Fools and Horses*. It meant that David only spent a week with us in rehearsal and a couple of days watching us in the show, before he acted John's part for two shows. No one in the company was disappointed by his performances as he is such a class actor.

I rehearsed on the Monday before the company arrived and then with them at 5 p.m. When I got to my dressing room on the Tuesday, they had decorated my door and my mirror and there were cards and welcome messages dotted all over the room. They were signed by everyone in the company welcoming me on board. Such friendship and kindness put me at ease. I had worked with Sophie Lawrence in pantomime in the Nineties and I respect her greatly. She's a fabulous actor, not just on soaps such as *EastEnders*, but also on stage.

The show went well and it wasn't too much of a baptism of fire for me, what with so much support from Sophie and the others. I didn't have a huge part, but Jeffrey Holland would stand by the door every night before I went on stage just to make sure I had the right cues.

Whilst the cast ensured that *Run for Your Wife* was an enjoyable experience for me, it was still more nerve-wracking than pantomime. In a play you really have to make sure that you are spot on with your cues, as in this play my cues were flying to a whole roomful of people. In drama there is some room for flexibility, but you always have to get the lines right. People often talk about actors adlibbing in pantomime, but what they don't realise is that you know your script so well that you can always go off script and return to the anchor of the text. There is a greater degree of flexibility in pantomime. The director will say, "I want you to get on at A and off at G but what you do in between is your business. I trust you because you know your craft." Acting in *Run for Your Money* was a totally different craft altogether. Even though my part was small I still had to get it right.

A few years later, I received a phone call from Peter Richards, the director of the highly-rated Fluellen Theatre Company which is based in Swansea, asking if I would like to act in a play called *Toshack or Me!* I can honestly say that this play changed my life, because from that moment on, people started talking about Kevin Johns, the actor. I have been saddled with a number of descriptions. There is Kevin Johns the DJ, which I loathe; Broadcaster Kevin Johns; Entertainer Kevin Johns; Comedian Kevin Johns; Local Celebrity Kevin Johns. I suppose as long as they say Kevin Johns, I don't care... unless it's DJ Kevin Johns.

Suddenly, people were talking and writing about me as 'comedy actor Kevin Johns' or sometimes just plain 'actor Kevin Johns'. I felt I had achieved something important.

Toshack or Me! changed my life in two ways. First, it got me more established as an actor, and second, it brought the Vicar Joe character into my life. Over the years, I had heard actors talk about how they had grown to love certain characters they played and they talked about the fictitious creations as if they were real. I have grown to love Vicar Joe and talk about him in a similar way.

Everyone thought that the character was based on me, but it wasn't. It just happens that like Vicar Joe, I used to be a minister of religion and absolutely adore football. In fact, Vicar Joe existed before the playwright, Peter Read, had even met me. I like to think that I have made the character my own and I would fight to the death to stop anyone else playing him.

As I say, the character brought me into the wonderful theatre company, Fluellen, for which I have worked several times since. The play, which was premiered in September 2006 at The Swansea Grand Studio Theatre, was a sell out every night and then transferred to the main auditorium in January 2007, where it also played to full houses. A year later it was reprised again! It came back as a result of public demand and it's not often that you can say that about a play. What was also exciting was to realise that about 70% of those huge audiences were new theatre-goers who were there because it was a play about Swansea City.

The other members of the cast and I felt that we were theatre missionaries. We were hoping that all those members of the audience who had never been to the theatre before would pick up leaflets and come and see future shows. It was wonderful hearing them talk before curtain up. They called the box office a ticket office and the interval half-time. The audience (or should I say the fans!), created a fabulous atmosphere. It was such a wonderful play in which to act.

I'm like Vicar Joe because he's a rebel, but I believe he is a rebel *with* a cause. There are people in life who are rebellious just for the sake of being rebellious. I would say that I have gone through that phase in my life. However, I think there is still a role for the rebel, as there are many times when we feel we have to challenge situations and attitudes. You could say it's a very biblical response, because in the Old Testament there is a passage that talks about the valley of dry bones. The people had become parched because they just didn't move with the times. It's often important to say to people, "Look, just because we've always done it this way doesn't mean we have to carry on."

On one occasion a lady came to me with a grievance. She informed me that she was a pillar of the Church. I told her, "Mrs Davies, if you are a pillar then you obviously don't move. Also, coming from a theatrical background, I must tell you that sitting behind a pillar can be absolute murder. Such a seat is often dubbed restricted vision. So, you are telling me you won't move and you have restricted vision?"

There are many elements of Vicar Joe's character which I share, although he's a drinker and I am not. As far as I'm concerned he has way too many drinks for his own good! There is a wonderful line in the play where he says, "Jesus turned water into wine, but the Church has done something far more difficult; it has turned wine into water." I, too, have grave concerns about the ways of the modern Church.

I am also like Vicar Joe in that I am a passionate football fan. I am afraid that like Vicar Joe, I have made excuses and missed vital appointments so I could be at a football match. I didn't miss my wedding, but I did go walkabout twice.

On the morning of my marriage to Rosie, my grandmother thought I had chickened out of the day. After the service, we were due to have a meal and I had been entrusted with the task of buying the drinks. I went to Asda in Llandudno and on my way back, not being superstitious in any way, I called in to see Rosie who was having her hair done at a friend's house and getting ready for the ceremony. The friend's son was playing football on the street outside. I had to join in and have a game, because as all fans will know, if there is a football within sight, it has to be kicked. I became so engrossed in the game that I was very late getting back, and my grandmother was convinced I had called off the wedding.

At the end of the reception, when the photographer was lining every one up for the last few photos, someone said, "Hang on a minute, where's Kevin?" Kevin was outside the church in his car, listening to Radio Wales Sportstime, trying to get the Swans' result. I am sure that Vicar Joe would have done the same!

In the play there is the wonderful story where Vicar Joe refuses to marry a Swans' fan to a follower of Cardiff City, because Joe doesn't believe in mixed marriages. When I learnt that passage, part of me thought, "Well, there's nothing wrong with that!" Learning the lines and playing the part, it became clear that the character had a passion for truth and football and a real love for people. I share all those preoccupations, but especially the latter. My love for people is what motivates me in all the different things I do.

Straight after playing Vicar Joe in *Toshack or Me!*, I

went into rehearsals for a show written by Mal Pope, called *Amazing Grace*. It was a musical based on the Welsh Religious Revival of 1904. The production was directed by the internationally famous Michael Bogdanov. I had been offered a part by his company the previous year, but the play was going to run at the end of the football season. Since the Swans had made the League One play-offs under Kenny Jackett, I didn't want to miss any vital games. This time, the play was due to open at the Swansea Grand Theatre in November 2006 and would then tour throughout Wales. As there were no vitally important games at that time of the year, I accepted the part!

I was cast as Will Hay, who was the leader of the Miners' Union. He worked in the same mine as Evan Roberts, the leader of the revival, and Evan's father and brother. For me it was an amazing part to be given, as I live so near to where the story was set. Evan was born in Loughor which is just a stone's throw from Kingsbridge, where I live. My house is on the same road as Moriah Chapel, where the Roberts family worshipped and where the revival started. Every day, I walk my dogs past Pisgah Chapel which Evan built to be used as a Sunday School and Young People's church during the revival. I am part of that community where it all happened. I have also met old people who knew Evan Roberts when they were children.

It is very strange that although I support – with one or two minor reservations – what Evan Roberts did, I was cast as one of the two main protagonists in the play. The other was the Reverend Peter Price, who dismissed the religious revival as a movement with little substance, based on mass hysteria. Peter Price was brilliantly played by Peter Karrie.

Although Will Hay believed in Christianity, he was much more committed to a social gospel. As a Christian I have no problem with that, because I think Christianity should be a blend of the spiritual and the quest for social justice. There are lines in the play where Will Hay states the number of miners who are killed every few weeks because of the atrocious conditions in the mine. He fought for better conditions, better pay, better rights and better care for his Union members. He couldn't understand why, instead of standing and fighting for a better world underground, many people were being distracted by spiritual goings on. That was the background to my character and it was a joy to play him and enter into his mindset.

Playing Will Hay every night, there were times when I felt a fraud in that I hadn't trained like all the others in the cast. To stand on the stage and sing in a trio with outstanding stars such as Sian Cothi and Peter Karrie was incredible. There were people who understood my own insecurities and said, "You've every right to be here because you've won it as a performer." It was a lovely company to be in, as there was a mixture of variety performers, dancers and actors. During the production there was even a ballet down the mines, which I have to admit, confused quite a few people.

While I enjoyed the experience and the feeling of being buoyed up by the support of others, it was also the hardest experience of my acting life. I was also doing my morning Breakfast Show, and during my time on air, I had to record my links for the last half hour. I would then leave the studio at half-nine, thirty minutes before the show ends, to be in Cardiff for rehearsals at ten-thirty.

When it was staged in Cardiff and Aberystwyth, I commuted by choice. I only took time off from the Radio Show for the week we performed in Llandudno. There was no way I could commute from Swansea to Llandudno every day, and I enjoyed going back to an area where I had been married and where my son was born. I loved walking in nearby Colwyn Bay, returning to where I had lived and worked.

It was also a pleasure to work with Michael Bogdanov, who is a great name in British Theatre. I remember the furore in the Eighties when he directed *Romans in Britain*. Personally, I don't believe in censorship, even if there are things happening in the world which are diametrically opposed to my beliefs. I think you win people over to your view by love; you don't convince them of your view by protesting.

A few years back the Grand staged *Shopping and F***ing*. A lot of people were surprised to see me there on the opening night. I had been asked to review the show for radio. I had to walk past lots of people from the Christian community to get into the building and past lots more who were inside the foyer, carrying out a silent protest. I finally arrived at my seat and saw the show. The essence of my review was:

"Some people will not like this play. I didn't. Some people will be offended by the play. I was. But instead of protesting against a play which has foul language and contains a gay rape scene, why not protest against a society which allows young men and women to go to London and be used by evil people?"

As far as I was concerned, the play was merely mirroring life.

On a totally different level, *Amazing Grace* managed to offend some people who felt it shouldn't have shown Evan Roberts' weaknesses. Yet he was a young man who was soon in the public eye, having received little training for the ministry. Although he died in the early 1950s, once the revival was over in 1904, he never spoke again in public or went to church. When he was ministering in Liverpool, it was clear that the man had had a severe nervous breakdown and found it impossible to speak to people who were from a culture which was totally alien to his. In the musical he is seen running away from the pulpit. The play also featured the fact that he had a great love in his life, a love that was never reciprocated. Mal's script was not afraid of depicting Evan's humanity and the temptations he endured.

What I found particularly interesting about doing the play was the fact that many of those involved in the production knew nothing about Evan Roberts. This led to many long and fascinating conversations with members of the cast between shows. In the show there is a scene where a fight breaks out. Two staunch left-wing miners went into a service in Bonymaen with the express purpose of disrupting the meeting. The build up to that fight was very emotional and for me, as a believer, I have to say that there were times in the play when I actually felt I was in a service. It was after such moments that discussions would break out amongst the production company. It all went to show that actors, dancers and performers are not as superficial as they are sometimes depicted.

Looking back on *Amazing Grace*, I think I grew as an individual during the run. That doesn't mean that everything went smoothly for me. I had some very difficult moments which came out of my own feelings of inadequacy and lack of confidence. In Aberystwyth we were still rehearsing certain scenes, especially one which featured me as Will Hay. The scene opens with Evan Roberts holding a prayer meeting in the mine. Hay is furious and asks, "What the hell is going on here? What do you think you're doing?" Hay challenges Evan about the terrible conditions in the mine and he wants to know why Evan is doing nothing to change the situation. Richard Munday (Evan Roberts) and I sing a duet called 'Always A Man Like You'. At the end of the song, I storm off.

On the Friday afternoon before the evening show we were still rehearsing this scene. The Associate Director had a go at me about the way I was performing. I don't know why, but I became so upset that I was on the brink. I thought, should I have a go at him and fight back or should I go outside the theatre and become emotional? I chose the latter option and went outside to phone home. As soon as I heard Rosie's voice, I cried. Aberystwyth Arts Centre where we were performing is on the University campus. So there I was, bawling my eyes out, surrounded by passing and intrigued students. I still find it difficult to decide whether my reaction was due to the emotion of the scene we had just done or to being pulled up on my acting.

When the Associate Director was told that I had ended up in this state, he was horrified. He apologised profusely.

"Kev," he said, "It's only a play. You have to learn to draw a line between reality and the work we're doing." The reason I had been challenged in the first place was because he wasn't too happy with my movement. I think because I come from a Variety background, my feet sometimes move more than they should. On one occasion Michael Bogdanov threatened to nail my feet to the stage!

Anthony Williams, the Associate Director who caused my floods of tears, is a first class choreographer. As a breed I think they are tough and they have to be very demanding of actors. You could publish a book on the one-liners I have heard attributed to them. I was once told that in a rehearsal, an actress fainted and was lying on the stage. The choreographer's direction to the rest of the cast was, "Dance around her, and when she comes around she can catch up."

That whole show was a great learning curve for me. When we staged it at the Millennium Centre in Cardiff I can remember standing behind the gauze and looking out at the huge audience of a couple of thousand. During the finale we led the audience in a song. As I stood there, hearing the swell of all those voices and thinking of the number of people who were there, I began to tell myself that I had come a million miles from doing a sketch on the streets of Watford.

The other big thrill of *Amazing Grace* came when we performed it at the Swansea Grand Theatre. My daughter, Bethan, who is now studying for a degree in Acting, and at the time was studying for a diploma in Performing Arts at Gorseinon College, was in the audience. She has seen me in hundreds of things over the years, but it was so wonderful when she came up to me and said, "Dad, I'm so proud of you."

My next acting role after *Amazing Grace* was playing the part of Vicar Joe again, this time in a play called *To Hull and Back* in February 2008. This was the sequel to *Toshack or Me!* and was based, as I previously mentioned, on the Swans' fight to stay in the Football League at the end of the 2002-3 season. For me, this play was a triumph. Peter Read, who had written *Toshack* when he didn't know me, this time wrote the Vicar Joe part with me in mind. There were eleven scenes in the play and I was in nine. I was rarely off stage and I hardly saw my dressing room except briefly in the interval and then in the curtain call.

Acting in the play was to be a huge challenge. When I saw how much I had to learn, I seriously wondered if I would make it. I came out of pantomime on the Sunday and started rehearsals for *To Hull and Back* on the Monday morning. I had to learn this new script as well as re-learn *Toshack or Me* for a one-off production before the sequel, all in ten days. In addition, I was doing my radio show every morning. It was an awesome task, but I did it because it was well-written and easy to learn. I may have put some things in the wrong order, but with Peter's plays you can do that.

He doesn't watch over you as a writer and say, "Ah, but you've missed out a comma or a full stop there." As long as you get the gist, he allows flexibility. There were some wonderful speeches and lines.

The play was very well researched and so easy to act. It was almost like one of those magic trick boxes I bought in my early days as a conjuror which would have the words 'No Skill Required' on the front. It was a great play to be in, and again it attracted huge audiences consisting mainly of Swans fans. My only disappointment is that because of the very nature of the script, the play can never go to a wider audience. I think Vicar Joe could travel and become a much-loved character in book form, play form or even on television. He could become a new Father Ted, because he is such a great creation.

A few weeks after *To Hull and Back* finished, I was back at the Grand Theatre playing various parts in Dylan Thomas' *Under Milk Wood* for the Fluellen Theatre Company. This was probably the most frightening experience of my life. I have to admit I didn't know the play particularly well. I grew up in an environment where everyone said that Dylan Thomas was the greatest writer to walk the earth. Inevitably, if you hear that long enough, you either accept it or rebel against it and I did the latter. Growing up, it was Dylan Thomas this, Dylan Thomas that, all the time. My grandfather went to the same school as the poet, so I also heard the adulation from him. He was also taught English by Dylan's father, D J Thomas. In Wales, if we can find a route to link us to someone who is famous, we'll take it. So, whilst

Above: With my mam (she's not the tall one) on a visit to Pinewood Studios.

Below: Rosie and I with Mam and Dad on our Wedding Day.

Above: With some
of the Match Day
Mascots before a
Swans game at the
Liberty Stadium.

Right: Bethan and
I rehearsing for the
Ballroom Dancing
Competition at
Theatre Penyrheol.
We won!

Above: We're very proud of Owain and Bethan. They've done okay! On a family break in Rome.

Below: Coats on! It was February in Rome. Rosie and I enjoying a beautiful city!

Above: Allan and
Wendie or Mam
and Dad.

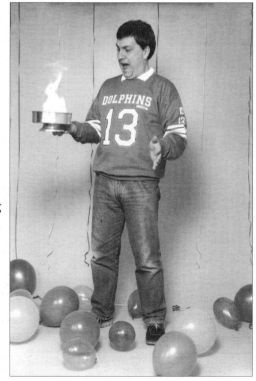

Right: Kev, a young
magician.

Right: Owain and I celebrating a title win at Rotherham – little did we know what had happened outside the ground.

Below: Abseiling for NCH Cymru off the top of Princess House in Swansea.

Me! In a ballet playing *La Fille De Mal Gardee* with Ballet Russe.

Pretty girls at the Swansea Sound Local Hero Awards.

Above: I love this job! With more pretty girls at the press launch of a show with *EastEnders* actress Hannah Waterman and the Marketing team from the Grand Theatre in Swansea.

Below: Not the best picture! I kept this because it shows the emotion that we felt after watching the Mia Tomlinson nomination DVD at the Local Hero Awards the year after she died. Mia won the Child of Courage Award in 2007 and died a few weeks later. We wanted to remember her at the 2008 awards.

Above: At Madame Tussauds in New York with comic hero Benny Hill.

Below: On the ferry to Liberty Island with my daughter Bethan on a family holiday to New York.

Above: I love Robin Williams! Perhaps this is as close as I'll get!

Below: This picture never made Katherine's book so I kept it for mine! I'm wearing the worst costume that I've ever been asked to wear.

Above: Rosie, Bethan and I in Bubba Gump's in Times Square.

Below: I love this picture taken at the Swansea Schools Music Festival.

Onstage as Joe, the Swans-loving Vicar, in *To Hull and Back*.

My daughter Bethan helping me get ready for my debut performance with Ballet Russe.

With dear friend Mike Doyle. We've appeared in five pantomimes together. I don't think there's a better non-double act in panto than Mike and me.

My favourite Dame role – Widow Twanky.

Above and facing page: PR Poses.

Bethan Thomas as Polly Garter with me as Rev Eli Jenkins in Fluellen Theatre Company's *Under Milk Wood* (2008).

it was drummed into me that my grandfather knew Dylan Thomas, in reality he would have had very little to do with him, unless Dylan, the Prefect, put him in detention, which I think is unlikely.

My research for playing the various roles in *Under Milk Wood* consisted mainly of lying on the bed reading the script and listening to a performance of the play on a CD. Peter Richards, the Director, had asked us not to listen to the Richard Burton production, so I found another one and listened to that instead!

As I listened to it, I began to see how funny it was. I also realised that many of the wacky characters Dylan created were similar to individuals I had known whilst growing up in Plasmarl. Willy Nilly, the Postman, the character I played, used to tell everyone what was in theirs and everybody else's post. Although my childhood postman, Cyril the Post, didn't steam people's mail open like Willy Nilly, he was a great character and got himself involved in everybody's life. If my mother found it difficult to get a parking space, she would often park her car on yellow lines to go into Princess House where she worked. Time and again Cyril the Post would run down the street shouting, "Wendie, Wendie, you've been booked again."

Under Milk Wood had Ocky the Milkman, we had Johns the Milk. It had Dai Bread, we had Noel the Bakehouse. Once I'd come to see that Dylan had created everyone's childhood village, I loved every minute of rehearsals and every minute of doing the show.

I decided to play Willy Nilly slightly camp, because I think any man who is that interested in gossip must be! I found the character of the Reverend Eli Jenkins very engaging, and when I came to play him I based him on a minister I once knew. I couldn't believe Eli's naivety. He stands listening to Polly Garter's song which celebrates the size of manhood possessed by the different men she had known. At the end of her musical rendition, the Reverend says, "O, Praise the Lord, for we are a musical nation." That is his response to a dirty song! Eli Jenkins loved people so much that he couldn't see anything wrong with the inhabitants of the town of Llareggub. I enjoyed playing him so much because here was someone who saw only the good in others, not the bad.

I was very nervous acting in *Under Milk Wood* because I felt I was putting myself up to be shot at. People could have said, "Who is this man with no formal training in acting, who's been a dame in pantomime and spins a few records on the radio (although, of course, we don't spin any more, because it's all computerised)? What's he doing playing all these parts in Dylan's home town in a production which puts a new spin on the play?"

Despite all those pre-play nerves, it was very well received. I understand some people were unhappy with the interpretation, but I think every time the play is performed it will divide audiences. Many have strong views on how it should be done, but Dylan Thomas died just a few weeks after its premiere in New York, so how can we know what he intended?

The other problem with any attempt to stage *Under*

Milk Wood is that it was intended for radio, not the stage. I thought we must have done something right when I heard two children walking out of an afternoon matinee and one of them said to the other, "I understand what it's all about now."

When we took it to Tenby, the audience laughed as freely as they had done two years previously when we had taken *Toshack or Me!* there. It was as if that audience had no preconceptions about how the play should be done, whereas I think Swansea audiences did. All over Wales, people claim Llareggub as their town. Perhaps it was The Mumbles or Laugharne. Who knows? In many ways it could be anywhere.

There are many wonderful lines which capture the essence of the Welsh people. My favourite is when one of the women says to her friend, "There's a lot of nasty people around here, mind." For some reason that line made me laugh every night and for me it captures something of the Welsh psyche.

In addition to acting on the stage, I was lucky enough to appear in the BBC Wales television production of *High Hopes*. On the way home from the audition, my mother rang me and I answered the call, hands-free, of course! She said, "How did you get on?"

"I got the part," I said.

"What is it?" she asked.

"I play a character called Geraint Flower."

"Is that a comedy part?" she asked.

"It's bound to be," I replied, "it's a comedy show." I always manage to say the wrong thing to my mother!

"Who is this character?" she asked.

"Mam," I replied, "he's a gay bingo caller." There was a long pause and then she said, "Well, make sure you don't tell anyone you're a bingo caller."

Strangely enough, before the offer of the part in *High Hopes*, I had been a bingo caller for one night only. I got myself into terrible trouble. Calling the numbers for Kev's Charity Flyer at Mecca Bingo Hall in Carmarthen Road, Swansea, I said, "One and one... " and before I could add the words, "makes two," most of the punters had filled in the number eleven on their cards.

That night I remembered an incident from my youth as a member of the City Temple Church on Alexandra Road. An old man used to stand up and pray the same prayer every service:

"We thank you, O Lord, that tonight we are not in the pubs, we are not in the clubs, we are not in the picture halls, the theatre halls or the bingo halls, but we are in the House of God."

On one occasion, he started praying in 1975 and finished the following year in 1976. It was a Watch Night service, and whilst he was still at prayer, the bells of the Police Station were ringing and the men from the Working Men's Clubs were singing 'Auld Lang Syne' on the street. He was thanking God that we were not in the pubs or the clubs, and the young people were looking at their watches wishing that they had been, because they would be home by now!

On the night I was the bingo caller for charity, I remembered his prayer. That night I completed the whole set. I had worked in theatres, clubs, cinemas and bingo halls. I had worked in every place he had prayed against, hopefully with a positive attitude.

CHAPTER NINE

Comic Belief

AFTER LEAVING BIBLE COLLEGE in June 1984, I went into the Ministry. My first church was in Garston, Liverpool. It was not a particularly good time to move to the area as it was three years after the riots which had ravaged the Toxteth area of the city.

Rosie and I became conscious of the great changes that were going on in Liverpool. It was the year that the city played host to the Garden Festival and they were redeveloping the Albert Dock. The first major event at the dock was a carol service in 1984 and I was asked to lead the singing, along with The Spinners.

As I made my first car journey from the city centre through Toxteth, Aigburth and out to Garston, I began to think, "What on earth have I come to?" It certainly wasn't Liverpool at its best. The changes that were taking place were cosmetic. It's interesting that Michael Heseltine was not universally loved because of his strong associations with Margaret Thatcher. Despite this, he was held in great affection by many Liverpudlians because he had poured money into the city in his capacity as Cabinet Minister for the Environment.

Our time in Birkenhead was enjoyable, as it was almost like being back in college. Rosie and I weren't married at the time, so we lived in separate flats in a huge old hospital which had been taken over by the Elim Church. It was called the Wirral Christian Centre. They ran a luncheon club and part of the building was a residential home. Pete and Julia Clothier lived there and they were particularly kind to Rosie. Although they were a recently married couple, they allowed her to stay with them in their part of the complex.

Leo and Hazel Mackleberg, who had been close friends of ours at college, were also living in the same building. Rosie often helped with the luncheon club and the nursing home, as her way of saying thanks for the opportunity of staying in the building.

Although my church was in Garston, I did quite a lot of work for the centre. I helped with their youth work and also with their Street Programme, helping drug users and prostitutes. It was an eye-opener for me. When I arrived in Liverpool, I wouldn't have been able to tell you the difference between sherbet and heroin. I was sent on a course and I learnt the hard way by spending a lot of my time with hardened drug users. We encountered people in desperate situations, and although we didn't have many breakthroughs, we saw some successes.

One young girl who was a single mother, had become involved with drugs despite coming from a respectable family. She was constantly arrested for shoplifting. Before one of her sprees, she had asked us, "Is there anything I can get you? I'm taking orders for Christmas." She handed us a list with all kinds of exotic foods and presents on it. What she didn't make clear was that she and her friends would go out and shoplift to order. She was charged with stealing annuals from Asda. We went to the court hearing and the magistrate told her, "If you appear before me again, then you will go to prison. Go with these people, listen to them and put your life in order."

One night I was driving back home through the Wallasey Tunnel, because the Birkenhead Tunnel was often closed at night for maintenance work. To get home I had to go through the docks, and near a level crossing was a notorious pub. Opposite was a small industrial estate where the Birkenhead prostitutes plied their trade. I saw the young girl standing on the corner. I was absolutely furious, because despite the fact that we had worked so hard with her, she was back on the streets.

I stopped the car and talked to her for a while. For a couple of weeks, she had been unable to get hold of drugs in Birkenhead as there had been a real clamp-down by the Police on drug trafficking. She'd heard that someone was doing a drugs drop that night on one of the estates. She asked me to take her there, but I couldn't. She was a lovely girl who had resorted to working as a prostitute to pay for her drug habit.

We encountered a fellow from New Brighton. He had been a family man who had started taking cannabis and then progressed to harder drugs. By the time we met him he had lost the use of his left arm and was living in a flat where all the windows were boarded up. We were asked if we could help in any way. He was in a terrible state. He was so weak he didn't have the strength to open tins of food. We would go down in the morning and open them for him.

One night in the North End of Birkenhead we were doing a drama presentation in one of the churches. The man promised to come to the presentation but didn't show up, so I went around to his flat. I managed to get in and discovered him collapsed on the floor. He was taken into hospital. When I brought him back to his flat, I asked him, "How did you end up like this? You are so dependent on the drugs."

"Kev," he replied, "I just wanted to be happy." We managed to get him into a rehabilitation home which would care for him.

Now that I am a professional actor and broadcaster, people are often intrigued as to why I hang on to my church connections. I would say it is because of people like the two I have just mentioned. I feel I have to continue working in the Church so that I can help people like them, who are damaging themselves in the pursuit of 'happiness'.

When it was announced in my church in Swansea that I had been accepted as a minister and was going to work in Liverpool, there was a mixed reaction. I overheard one man tell a large group of churchgoers, "Well, he's the last person I would expect." In many ways, I suppose I am, but I have always believed that God chooses the fools of this world to confound the wise.

Despite my rebellious nature and reputation, I was the first person from my year in Bible College to start in a church, just two weeks after graduation. The church in Garston had a small congregation and they had obviously appointed me in the hope that I would attract newcomers. I was able to do that, but keeping them was a different matter. I must admit I was not so good at teaching them the rudiments of the faith in those days.

Rosie and I were able to help many individuals with their social and practical problems. We would often receive phone calls late at night from people who were feeling suicidal or in desperate need of a shoulder to cry on. The church members were extremely kind to us and supportive, although I felt they needed someone who would focus just on them.

One day, I was contacted by Radio Merseyside and asked to appear on one of their programmes. I think they had heard of me because I was constantly putting articles and news items into the press, as part of my strategy to raise the church's profile. The presenter was also interviewing two other people. One was heavily involved in Liverpool's Garden Festival and the other was a female singer who had just returned from entertaining in The Falklands. He introduced us as three of the most influential young people on Merseyside. That proved to me that I had made some kind of splash in the community, even if it hadn't percolated through to the congregation.

Then, I was asked to lead an Elim Church in Colwyn Bay. When I moved from Garston, I had to pull over onto the hard shoulder of the M53 because tears were streaming down my cheeks. I realised that despite the difficulties, I was leaving some good new friends behind.

If my time in the church in Garston had been tough, then the new one in Colwyn Bay was to prove even tougher. The church had been closed for a couple of months and I was staying in a winter let which was really kitted out for the summer. It was freezing there. I was on my own as at that stage I had not yet married Rosie. The meters all seemed to be programmed to give you the least amount of heat. On arrival, I spent a few days visiting people in the area, especially those who had attended the church in the past.

On the Friday before the opening Sunday service in February 1985, I drove down to my old college in Capel for a meeting. Afterwards, I offered to drive an old college friend back to Dudley in the Midlands. By the time we got onto the M1 it started to snow. Once we arrived in the town, the snow was very thick and there was no way I could drive on to north Wales. I stayed the night with my friend and in the morning, whilst there was still a huge covering of snow on the ground, I thought it would be safe to make the trip back home. I needed to get back as I had a sermon to write for the important opening service the next day. I started driving and I telephoned my father from a service station.

"You fool," he said, "I've listened to the weather forecasts and the predictions are horrific." There was nothing I could do about the situation; I had to press on. I found that the further north I went, the thicker the snow became.

I reached Birkenhead and decided to stay in my old flat there, as I had only moved away a fortnight earlier and still had the key. The idea was that I would set out in the morning for Colwyn Bay, which under normal circumstances, would take just over an hour. I heard that someone I knew had driven up to Holyhead, which is further north than Colwyn Bay, so I thought, "If he can make it, I'll be fine." I set out immediately on the A55, the north Wales link road, and didn't see a single car. There were none to overtake and none on the other side of the dual carriageway. The snow was banked up on both sides of the road and I began to wonder whether the road was open!

The following morning, I arrived at the church in time for the momentous first service, only to discover that no one else had made it. I was the only one in the church. It was an incredibly short sermon, the singing was terrible and the collection was pathetic, but at least I opened the doors that Sunday morning, and it took off from there.

In the time that we were there, dozens of new people joined us. By the time of the first Christmas Carol service, we had moved from the zero attendance of the blizzard service to a congregation of a hundred. We were there for three years and in that time we saw the church grow numerically. Some stayed, while others moved on to other churches for more intense teaching. I didn't mind that because I saw my role as a 'bring 'em in' pastor.

Colwyn Bay has always had a special significance for us. It is where Rosie and I were married, where we set up our first home together and where our son, Owain, was born

– in the HM Stanley Hospital in St Asaph. So, despite his frequent protestations that he is a 'Swansea Jack', in reality he is a 'Gog', because he was born in north Wales and didn't move to the promised land of Swansea until he was four months old.

When Bethan was born in Morriston Hospital, Swansea, the nurse asked if I had any other children. When I told her about Owain, she wanted to know in which hospital he was born. I answered HM Stanley, and she thought I had been in the Navy. Lots of people think Owain's birthplace is a ship, rather than a hospital named after the 'Doctor Livingstone, I presume?' Stanley.

As I have already mentioned, I have a passion to see Wales united. I think it is sad to see and hear so much antagonism between the North and South of the country. In a small way, our two children bring together the warring factions. I also have to say that I have a love for both parts of Wales. Although I spent much of my youth on the Gower beach at Llangennith and Crawley Woods, my favourite places in Wales are Morfa Nefyn on the Llŷn Peninsula and Llanberis, both of which are in the north. Rosie worked in Bather's bakery in Colwyn Bay, and when we both had free time, we would put the dog in the car and drive to these beauty spots.

When we got married in Colwyn Bay, we spent the first night in Llandudno. The next morning, I preached in the church in Colwyn Bay, but it was a very short sermon! On the Sunday night we stayed in a hotel in Norfolk Square in London. It was the only hotel I knew in London. I'd stayed there before, and as it was run by a Welsh couple, I knew that we would be looked after well. For the remainder of the honeymoon, we stayed around the corner from Arsenal Football Club's old ground at Highbury with our friends, Martin and Meg Wroe. They were fantastically hospitable and gave us a great time.

We went to the Houses of Parliament where we were shown around by Sir Anthony Meyer, the MP for Clwyd West, a constituency which included Colwyn Bay. As well as seeing a pantomime at the London Palladium starring Dame Anna Neagle and Paul Nicholls, we saw an outlandish play at the Drill Hall. After that performance we were running out of money, so we decided to go back home. We didn't tell anyone we were returning and had a day to ourselves in Colwyn Bay.

The first thing we did was get a dog from the Animal Rescue. I think Rosie was expecting a Golden Labrador with a six months' supply of toilet paper, but instead we came away with a beautiful puppy. At first Rosie wasn't sure, but as soon as she rolled on her back (the dog, not Rosie), she fell in love with the animal. We had Cindy for fourteen and a half years.

We were in the church in Colwyn Bay for three years. I received offers to pastor other churches, and we thought long and hard about our next move. I was anxious to be released into a more itinerant ministry, working with children in the community and also in schools. I needed to know what to do.

One of the options was to bring in another person to run

the church while I worked away, using Colwyn Bay as my base. I didn't think that would be fair on the new minister. We were living in the church manse, so that would have raised the question of where he would stay. Besides, the church wouldn't be able to afford two salaries. In fact, they couldn't afford one! Another option was to move back to Birkenhead. There were a number of churches across the country which were keen for me to use them as my base.

After much thought, we decided to move back to Swansea. In some ways the move didn't turn out as we had anticipated. I travelled the length and breadth of the country and abroad doing itinerant Christian work. Our minister in Swansea suggested that we move to Birmingham, which from the point of its centrality, was a sensible suggestion, but it also made me wonder whether he was trying to tell me something else! As we had no contacts in that area, we decided to stay put.

It was difficult to feel part of anything, because every Sunday I would be at the other end of Britain. The day after we moved into our new house in Swansea, I left Rosie with all the bags unpacked, jumped in the car and drove to Coventry to work there. There were times when I was away from home for up to a month.

People often worry about me and tell me that I am doing too much, but that is the way I am. I have a tremendous zest for life and a huge amount of energy. Sometimes, though, my body tells me to stop, and on those occasions I take to my bed. When that happens, I have a temperature and feel as though I've caught something viral. I can't eat or do anything, and stay in bed for a day or two before bouncing back. Fortunately, this happens less often now than in the past.

1992 saw the end of my formal ministry. This left me free to pursue full-time work with Swansea Sound Radio. I was convinced that I had made the right move in seeking my future in the entertainment world, whilst keeping my links with the Church. The only time I had a serious doubt about whether I had made the right decision, was when Premier Radio, a London-based Christian station, contacted me. They asked me to send them some material and to name the salary I would expect. That approach did give me a slight wobble and I momentarily wondered if I was on the right track.

Eventually, I decided to stay put in Swansea, and for the next year or two I did a combination of children's entertainment, plus work for Christian organisations such as Tear Fund and Spring Harvest. I also did some work for the Anglican Church in Wales. They approached me on a couple of occasions to say that there might be a job for me in the future. I decided against that because I didn't know the lines or the moves, but I did like the costumes!

I am aware that some people within the Church are confused by my position and unsure where to place me, but I'm Kev and I'm happy being me. I would describe myself as a passionate Christian believer who wants to bring about change in society. I'm shaped by my faith and not the institutionalised Church.

For example, when we were in Colwyn Bay, a young

mother who had very little money came to the manse with her son. Later that day Rosie and I went shopping and took her two boxes of groceries plus some comics for the little lad. In the same town, we used to visit the laundrette which was run by a man in his seventies. On Christmas Day we made an extra meal for him because we knew he'd be on his own. He was so touched. His reaction and that of the mother reminded me there are many ways to show Christianity in action, other than through the pulpit.

Although I love Wales deeply, I am glad that I have experienced life outside the country. Travelling around has helped me meet a diversity of people – not least Rosie, who is from Scotland. These meetings have taught me that people are exactly the same, with the same worries and fears, the world over. There are good people and bad people everywhere. I have a huge passion for people wherever I meet them. I've loved meeting the locals in places such as Romford, Dagenham and Chelmsford. I also love those from the North West of England. In the Midlands, Birmingham is a city that excites me.

I once spent a week in Glasgow, staying with a fellow who worked for Glasgow City Mission. I was working in a church in the Gorbals, which is one of the most notorious parts of the city. He asked me to accompany him on a late night soup run. I thought I had better say yes, even though I was very tired, having just arrived from north Wales by train. I had also just done a session at a church in Glasgow. Despite the fatigue, I asked myself, "How can I say no, when this bloke is going out to do a shift with homeless street people?"

I saw things that night which frightened me to death. Not in terms of scary situations, but wondering how people could live in such terrible circumstances. Near a bus station, a cleaner told us that earlier that night he had seen a homeless couple who were so drunk, they hadn't realised another man was trying to molest their fifteen-year-old daughter. The cleaner had chased him away with his brush. I saw homeless people fighting over who should sleep closest to the hotel vents to benefit from the hot air. There are great divides in Glasgow, but through my visits there I have learned to appreciate all sides.

I know people on both sides of the sectarian divide in Belfast. They are slowly beginning to understand that there is far more to unite them than there is to divide them. They all want good education for their children, they want freedom and to be able to walk the streets in safety.

Travelling around Britain in that period of my life, from 1984 to 1994, I met many people and I saw good in all of them. That was probably when I fell in love with people – with the excitement of meeting them and sharing their experiences. I want that openness in the Church. I can't stand the 'nuclear bunker' mentality that says, "We'll hang on in here until the end of time."

My fear of Judgement Day is that I will be accused of not using the talents I've been given. I stand in two worlds because I want to bring those two worlds together. I try and do this through my cabaret show, *Comic Belief*. It combines humour with faith and it's been running since 2003. The show gives churches an opportunity to invite people to a dinner or informal evening where I tell some of the stories which are in this book. It is a chance for me to share my life in a way which is fun and non-threatening.

I never wanted to be Chaplain of Swansea City Football Club. A very good friend of mine in Swansea, Glyn Davies, invited John Bowyer, Chaplain of Manchester United, to come to Swansea. I'd met John when I was in Bible College and he was a minister in Watford. Glyn had organised John's trip to explore the possibility of sports chaplaincy in Wales. I arranged for a meeting to be held in the Hospitality Room at the Vetch. The audience was mainly comprised of people interested in sport from churches across the city. The following day we had an event at Loughor Rugby Club, where some of the Swans' players came and took part in quizzes. On the Sunday we held a football tournament at the old Morfa Stadium with several church teams taking part. At the end of those three events we explored the possibility of sports chaplaincy in Swansea.

The Swans stated that they didn't want a chaplain, saying, "We have Kev and anything we need doing, Kev can do it." Just a few weeks after that, I led the prayers for Terry Cole and his family after the match at Rotherham. So I started fulfilling the role of chaplain without anything being official.

After the club was saved from ruination under Petty, David Morgan from the Board of Directors wrote to me and said, "Thanks for all your help and support." At the end of the letter there was the usual statement saying that I should contact them if there was anything they could do for me. So I said, "Dave, have a word with the Board and encourage them to appoint a chaplain." Soon after that, I received a letter stating that the Board were delighted to invite me to be the Chaplain for Swansea City Football Club. I wondered if I had the time to fulfil the task. I also wondered whether people would relate to me as a chaplain, because they relate to me mainly as a performer.

One of the misconceptions about sports chaplains is that they deal only with the players. Most of the players are young men at their physical peak and earning good sums of money. Such people rarely think that they need help. My role has been to be there for them if they need me, but also to help supporters and office staff who are going through difficult times.

Some chaplains like to go out and train with the team. I am not one of them! However, one day I decided I would go down to the Vetch and train with the Youth Team. At the end of the session, I was formally introduced to the players. I said to them, "Any problems, any difficulties, anything you want to talk about, give me a ring."

A couple of weeks later when I was playing the Dame at the Swansea Grand Theatre, I walked into the market in costume to adjudicate the best-dressed stall for Christmas. It's a difficult task which calls for the Wisdom of Solomon and the speed of an athlete to escape once you have announced the result. As I walked in to the market hall, I heard a whistle. I regularly get wolf whistles when I walk around as the Dame, but I normally ignore them. On this occasion I turned around to see Antonio Corvascerri and Stuart Jones from Swansea City Youth Team. They said, "Any problems, any difficulties, anything you want to talk about, give us a ring!"

CHAPTER 10

Still Making Sense of it All

Looking back on my life so far, I've enjoyed everything that's happened. When you become well-known, I suppose people want a slice of you. In many ways I am lucky that my fame territory is the SA postal code, as well as part of CF. It must be difficult for mega-celebrities who can hardly move and have to be careful of what they do and say. I enjoy the fact that people stop me on the street or in Tesco's and want to chat. As a performer, I would have more of a problem if every time I went out, no one recognised or talked to me.

I am never depressed about the way things develop and I think that is because I never set out to be a celebrity. I worry when people tell me that they have decided to go on programmes such as *The X Factor*. You watch them on television pleading with the organisers, "Oh, please give me a chance. I want it more than anything in the world. Please, please, let me go through."

All they want is to be famous. As far as I am concerned they have the wrong motivation. It's not a matter of being famous, but more a question of earning a living from start to finish.

I know a young boy who auditioned for one of the *Pop Idol* series, but didn't get through. So then he did it the right way by going to college and training. He is now a potential big name in the West End.

As a performer, I worked hard to achieve what I have. Like many other people I did my apprenticeship in church halls, beach clubs, social clubs and other places a million miles from the glare of TV cameras. If something big comes along, then of course, I will take it, but I am happy with the way things are.

What has galvanised me is that, whenever I have attempted something, there was always someone telling me I would never achieve my goals. Once you tell me I am incapable of doing something, I will use all my energy and talent to prove you wrong. I learnt in Dynevor School from a couple of inspirational teachers that it was important to chase rainbows. I like to surround myself with positive people. A friend once told me, "If you want to fly with eagles, don't walk with turkeys."

My family were never negative and they always encouraged me to go as far as I could in everything I attempted. Rosie has been terrific, because when we were married she had no idea that she was taking on an entertainer with all the demands that would bring. At first she thought we would be committed to a life in the Church and Christian ministry together. The whole idea was that we would share this calling. Instead of that she has suddenly become the wife of an entertainer who is constantly in the public eye.

As a performer, I have always re-invented myself. Whatever my hopes and ambitions were as a teenager, the early public perception of me was as a clown. Since then I have gone through several reincarnations: broadcaster, pantomime Dame, and comedian; now I feel I have come to where I wanted to be in the first place, a stage actor. All these changes have reinforced my belief that you have to keep moving to keep working.

Whilst I am ambitious, I am also content. Years ago I bought a Land Rover Discovery. I loved the car but for a long time I wondered whether the boy from Plasmarl was reaching above his station. When the head gasket blew, the car was off the road for several weeks. With the cost of repair and the heavy petrol consumption, I decided to buy a Skoda Octavia. When they first hit the market, Skodas were something of a joke, but I am now the proud owner of one and I became even prouder when I realised I had driven it from Swansea to Euro Disney in Paris on one tank of petrol. Many people are after bigger and better houses and cars, but I am happy with what I have.

Despite my contentment, I sometimes wonder whether I am a pioneer who has become a settler. There is a very thin line dividing that sentiment from the phrase: 'a rolling stone gathers no moss'. Sometimes I am surprised that I have been in the one place for so long. I still have this yearning to go off and do new things. I now understand why some actors would want to walk out of a soap opera, despite the fact that they have an £80,000 salary, plus an extra two or three thousand pounds every time they open a supermarket or a night club.

When I returned to Swansea in 1987, I didn't think I would still be here twenty years later, but I love Swansea and I love its people. I suppose I have come to terms with the fact that pioneering is not just a matter of geographical movement. I can still drive things forward and bring in new initiatives in the place where I was born and have lived for so many years. There is still a lot more for me to pursue and achieve.

I think the variety of my life feeds the comedy and also helps me as a broadcaster. For example, when I visit Greenock in Scotland, where Rosie was born, I have to confess that I am often unsure of what people are saying to me because of their strong accent. I also struggle with the linguistic differences. On one occasion I went into a baker's shop and asked for a pasty. The shop assistant looked confused and said she didn't sell pasties. When I pointed to the scores of pasties on a tray in the shop window, she said, "Oh, you mean a bridie." She placed it on a paper tissue and I winced when I held it, because it was very hot.

"Would you like a wee poke with that?" she asked. I looked anxiously around at other people and replied, "The shop's very busy and we've not been introduced." I discovered afterwards that a poke is a bag.

What I like about my work is the tremendous unpredictability every day. I was asked to compere an afternoon dance show at the Swansea Grand Theatre. I was looking forward to it because of my love for dance and the fact that it involved schools. I put on my best suit and arrived for the lunchtime event. I soon realised I was dressed inappropriately because it was a street Hip Hop dance competition. I had to think quickly, and as there was no way I could change my clothes, I decided to introduce the competition wearing my suit and a baseball cap on backwards!

I am very excited when I see people who I introduced as youngsters in talent shows, now succeeding in the world of show business. People such as Craig Gallivan, who starred in *Footballers Wives*, and Nia Jermin. They have worked so hard to get where they are today, and nothing gives me greater pleasure than to see youngsters who were once unknown performers enjoying the limelight.

I hope that my two children, who I believe are incredibly gifted individuals, will exceed what I have achieved. At the moment they are introduced as Kevin Johns' daughter or son. I look forward to the day when people say of me that I am Owain Johns' father or Bethan Johns' dad! The role and support of my family has been so crucial in the rollercoaster ride I have endured and enjoyed so far.

I end where I began: I live with the fear of failure. Although I have acted to full theatres and a packed Millennium Centre, I still remember that I have not had Drama School training. And there are always those who want to shout out, "You're just a clown." I'm not ashamed of my clowning, but I wonder why they say it.

Even in the Church I used to feel slightly out of things. I've never lost my faith but I've sometimes wondered if I've got it wrong. I don't look spiritual, nor do I dress or speak spiritually.

At the end of the day, though, I'm happy with who I am and what I've done. And all I can say to people is... this is me!

Oh Yes It Is... Kevin Johns!

Also published by Y Lolfa

The autobiography of El Gaffer, *Kicking Every Ball*
follows his career from his early days in Catalonia, to
playing in the Spanish league, moving to Wigan as one
of the 'Three Amigos', and finally to Swansea where he
flourished as a player before dominating as a manager.

He also reflects on the fantastic 2007/08 season and
the road to the Championship.

Available at your local bookshop, at the Liberty
Stadium, from Amazon, and also direct from the
publishers.

ISBN: 978 1 84771 085 7
Fully illustrated hardback, £12.95

ROBERTO

KICKING EVERY BALL
My Autobiography

y Lolfa

This book is just one of a whole range of
publications from Y Lolfa. For a full list of
books currently in print, send now for your
free copy of our new full-colour catalogue.
– or simply surf into our website

www.ylolfa.com

for secure on-line ordering.

TALYBONT CEREDIGION CYMRU SY24 5AP
e-mail ylolfa@ylolfa.com
website www.ylolfa.com
phone (01970) 832 304
fax 832 782